Books by Gerald Green

THE PORTOFINO P.T.A.

THE HEARTLESS LIGHT

THE LOTUS EATERS

THE LAST ANGRY MAN

THE SWORD AND THE SUN

HIS MAJESTY O'KEEFE
(with Larry Klingman)

the Portofino
P. T. A.

GERALD GREEN

the Portofino
P. T. A.

CHARLES SCRIBNER'S SONS • NEW YORK

for Nancy, Teddy, David
. . . and Marie

"This region (of Italy) is headquarters not only for the wealthy, the titled, the smart and the yachtsmen, but also for the literary set. . . . There are but a handful of spots in all the world of such concentrated beauty. Comparisons are invidious, inaccurate, unfair—true enough. But this cluster of resorts has an indescribable quality that brings to mind the isles of Capri: madly *chi-chi*, alluring, gay, snobbish and vibrant with something, a mood, that can't be defined but certainly can be felt. Be careful; it gets in your blood."

—Fodor's 1959 *Guide to Italy*

A few months after my third book, *The Last Angry Man*, was published, favorably reviewed (for the most part) and widely read, I began to be troubled by a recurrent nightmare.

In this dream, Grace Metalious (*Peyton Place*) marries Jack Kerouac (*On the Road*). The newlyweds then move into a large split-level house in a wealthy suburb—Great Neck, N.Y., Winnetka, Illinois, Westwood Village, California. Instead of planting azaleas and building retaining walls, the new residents do nothing but throw parties. None of the neighbors is invited. But the people that *are!* Norman Mailer, Françoise Sagan, Rona Jaffe—

Now the trouble is, Herman Wouk lives next door. After a week of these parties, with bongo drums going all night, and beer cans piling up in the rock garden, Wouk loses patience. He calls the City Zoning Commission, which is headed by James Gould Cozzens.

"This is a disgrace," Herman Wouk tells him. "The neighborhood is deteriorating with this new element. What happened to all the respectable people we used to have here, like J.P. Marquand and John O'Hara?"

Instead of answering him, Cozzens reads Wouk the history of the zoning regulations. "Our ancestors—*mine*, that is—planned wisely and well," he says, "in establishing a legal groundwork for those rules of conduct that govern all civilized men—"

Fascinating material, but no help to Wouk. A few days later Vladimir Nabokov rents an old Tudor House down the street and announces that he is forming a Brownie Troop. Wouk has no choice but to move. His lovely home is bought by Truman Capote.

What is disturbing about this dream, is that there is no role for me in it. I am always an observer, never a participant. Reluctantly, I came to the conclusion that I lacked identity. There remained no choice for me but to get out of the country, to seek myself in Europe. In the first chapter I will detail the steps that led us there, the folly that sent us scurrying to the Italian Riviera—and disaster.

The town we went to was Rapallo. It nestles in a stretch of rocky, piney seacoast called the *Riviera di Levante* (Eastern Riviera) 19 miles east of the great port of Genoa.

Rapallo is one of three towns which unite to form a resort hierarchy in northern Italy. The other two, as one travels west toward Genoa, are Santa Margherita Ligure and Portofino. Rapallo is the biggest and most stodgy—19,000 year-round inhabitants, the former home of Ezra Pound and Sir Max Beerbohm, site of the Treaty of Rapallo. Santa Margherita has about 12,000 permanent residents, is heavier on the *chi-chi,* and features an open fish market. Here, the local boats deliver their daily catch of squid, octopus, shrimp, porgy and other Mediterranean delicacies. Old ladies, barefoot, in black shrouds, will happily sell you a meagre flounder for six dollars. Beware of this market. Indeed, beware of Mediterranean fish. They are very boney, and one pays by the bone. Myself, I am a North Atlantic fish fancier. (Thank you, waiter, some more of those fresh Cherrystone clams, from a cool, pure Atlantic bed.)

Where the scenic road—and all illusions—come to a dead end, lies Portofino, the ultimate, the zenith of Italian resorts. It is more than a little fishing village taken over by the elite—it is a state of mind, a form of paranoia.

Portofino is tiny—a cleft in the rocky slopes, lined with crumbling docks and flaking old buildings, expensive shops, equally expensive restaurants, post card venders, and old ladies in black, selling walnuts and filberts strung like necklaces. The harbor is haven to a half-dozen millionaires' yachts and sight-seeing boats, run by cheerful Genovese pirates. High on the stone slopes, amid parasol pine and cypress, nest several dozen villas of the rich and powerful—Italian newspaper publishers, heirs to English land fortunes, Americans living on tax-free bonds.

The very name Portofino has become a symbol for the romantic, the exotic, the lavishly tranquil. Charm, beauty, quaintness, atmosphere and good wine are said to abound there. None of this is true. Portofino is best seen the way the sight-seeing busses laden with the *lumpen* middle-class of West Germany see it: an hour's stop for a bad lunch, then on to Rapallo. (Don't stay there, either. Proceed at once to Florence, where there is art, and life, and affirmation. Go to the *Bargello*—not on most of the guided tours—and be awed by the statues of Donatello and Mino da Fiesole).

Such is Portofino—the dream city of tourism. In Hollywood, there is a Portofino shop, where choreographers buy bulky sweaters at a price that would feed Albania for a month. There was once a bad Broadway musical called *Portofino;* a television series of the same name is imminent; there are dozens of Porto-fino night-clubs. An insipid wine labelled Portofino is marketed —distilled from indifferent grapes.

Portofino, then, is the ultimate fantasy of a Europe that has ceased to exist. Try to drive into Portofino on a Saturday night in August. At once, you are locked in bumper-to-bumper agony, as nerve-wracking as the Long Island Expressway on July 4th. You may spend three hours on the winding road—sweating, cursing, grinding gears. And since the road is hewn from the native rock, there is no place to make a U-turn or get off. Exhausted, you arrive in Portofino at midnight—and discover there is nothing to do. *Nothing.* The restaurants have closed. Perhaps an old lady selling walnuts is still awake. There is a snobbish little bar, on a moored barge, where you may pay two dollars for the privilege of sitting on an orange crate and drinking vermouth. By then it is time to disentangle one's car from the parking lot—I neglected to mention that the parking lot is two-thirds of downtown Portofino—and creep back to Rapallo.

There is no P.T.A. in Portofino.

CHAPTER one

why Italy?

Some kind of flickering light, a halation, surrounds my long bald head, and signals to the salespeople of the world: *sucker*.

Discount house clerks chuckle as I approach. They know, they know, that the three-way AM-FM TV-radio-phonograph that will never work properly (special sale, no guarantees) will inevitably be mine.

Once I bought a snappy little foreign car, much reduced in price because of inundation in a tidal wave. For the nominal sum of $200, the friendly dealer put it in running order—but the guarantee ended the moment I drove off. The following morning, my shrewd bargain refused to start. It still refuses to start, more often than not. What jolly fun in the sales room, when the boys reminisce about that big boob who bought the job with the permanently busted syncromesh!

Recently I bought a dog. Again, it was a "special deal." A friend had gotten a handsome beagle from a breeder in Vermont. Inquiries were made on my behalf. The breeder sent word he had an intelligent, lively male pup, for the same price my friend paid—a mere fifteen dollars. Buoyant, I motored to Vermont. Surprise! The beagle breeder also sold antiques. In the general good feeling, I let myself be talked into a Colonial relic, an alleged grain bin. It might have been Ethan Allen's coffin. It was a steal at $187.

Having made this killing, I was now ready to buy a beagle. Somewhere along the line, I had been misinformed. The dog was a female. It was not lively at all, but appeared to suffer from a trembling syndrome. Moreover, there had been an error in the reported price. The *real* price was $40. I complained about the dog's shiverings, but the breeder-dealer assured me it was normal. He wore shaggy tweeds and space shoes—no rustic bumpkin, he.

Cowed, I sped home with my two acquisitions. The beagle never stopped shaking. Neurotic, moody, it ran from our caresses, refused to eat, and killed a neighbor's duck—a crime of violence in Fairfield County. The dog now has gone to its reward—that Great Kennel in the Sky—by way of the Humane Society.

As for the grain bin, it served a brief apprenticeship in our living room, until its funerary shape so depressed my wife, that she banished it to the basement. There, bowed legs and all, it functions as a repository for canned beer.

These evidences of my general ineptitude in the ways of the

2

world are cited as relevant to our sojourn on the Italian Riviera. Of all men, I was surely the most unlikely to uproot my wife and my three small chicks—aged 6, 4 and 2—from their comfortable split-level development house, squatting on 76 x 100 feet of Long Island topsoil, and establish them on a wild Mediterranean seacoast.

Every time I make a bad move, or am euchred, or enticed into a bargain laden with snares, a soft voice tells me: *Let well enough alone. Seek no adventures. Avoid bargains. Stay where you are. Sit down, shut up and watch television.* Rarely do I heed the advice.

The exact moment at which I decided to go to Italy occurred on an August evening in 1958, in Westhampton Beach, Long Island. My wife and I were guests at a buffet supper at the lavish beach house of a theatrical agent. The agents own the biggest, most luxurious houses in Westhampton. The writers live in leaky hovels. That summer, I was still something of a hot item, after the success of *The Last Angry Man*. (Fame fleeth: I was later displaced by a young playwright who kept audiences spellbound with accounts of his horrid addiction to betel nut.)

That night, shivering in the Atlantic's frigid blasts, I fell in with a variegated group on the patio. There was a blonde television actress, an account executive who handled millions in fertilizer, and a cunning theatrical lawyer who assured me I had made every conceivable blunder with my literary earnings, and that he could have shown me twelve ways to cheat the government. It was a good, solid, group.

I sipped Coca-Cola (even the smell of alcohol induces migraine in me) and listened. Suddenly, the blonde actress, who had just met me, seized my tie, a modest silk repp from Rogers Peet, and dipped its lower half in her gin and tonic. Keeping it

3

thus immersed, she winked at the others, pointed at my innocent face and announced in a loud, clear voice:

"*Square!*"

The effect was instantaneous. All laughed, repeated her charge, shared a sense of revelation, of unfrocking. I saw the truth myself. I was square. There was no argument about it. Soon, the actress saw a television producer and released my soggy tie. The lawyer and the advertising fellow drifted away, and I was left alone, trembling in the ocean breeze. She was right. But *why* was she right? Why was I truly square—as opposed to oblong, circular, trapezoidal, or parallelepiped?

Nervously I checked my credentials. I had produced two successful television programs in the news and public affairs area—programs I had no reason to apologize for. I had written three books. I had a wife; three children; a house; two cars; two University degrees. More and more, as I studied myself, I realized how truly square I was. Everyone at that party knew it.

> Go tell it on the mountain
> Over the hills and everywhere!
> Go tell it on the mountain,
> That Gerald Green is square, Hallelujah!

But what exactly was it that made me square? My split-level house? My Plymouth—that squarest of cars? My affection for Joseph Conrad? It was none of these. It was the essential *me*. And I suppose that if I were the owner of a bowling alley, or an obstetrician, squaredom would have been irrelevant. For a writer, however, it is a portent of doom. My credentials were all wrong. Never had I worked as a stevedore, fruit picker, or light-weight boxer. Never had I earned a public reputation as a drunk, addict, lecher or *invertito*. I had always earned a living at a job—newspaper writer, television writer, etc. Liquor was alien to me. I am known to get a headache simply by looking at Macy's full-page booze ad in the *Times*. All those bottles!

To use talker jargon, I projected no public image. Consider Jack Kerouac. Every time Kerouac writes a book, the publicity attendant tells of his great ability as a football player at Columbia. His first book's dust jacket extolled him as 'a varsity player.' With his next, he was one of Lou Little's most promising backs. With his next he was the greatest half-back ever to play at Columbia. Finally, he was an All-American. Thus, as Kerouac's books get duller, his football prowess gets greater. Confounded, I once asked a friend who *was* an All-American at Columbia, just how good the Beatnik Beatus was. "He was a stiff," responded my friend. "He couldn't block."

In any case, there I was—a novelist in a split-level house, suffocating in squareness. A few days after my tie had been dipped, I confronted my wife, Marie, over the Kix. Like me, they floated—unable to plumb the literary depths. They were round, but I was square.

"I've had enough of this suburban nonsense," I said. "And some suburb! What's wrong with these people? Don't they read all those books about the corruption in the suburbs? We haven't been to a single wife-swapping party. No one's made an anti-Semitic remark. Worse, nobody's made a pass at you. I haven't seen a drunk here in five years. The house is well-made and fairly priced. We have to get out of here."

"What do you suggest?" asked Marie, forcing oatmeal between David's locked teeth.

I studied the TWA calendar on the door leading to the den. The *den!* We had planned it to be my study. Now it was a Kentiled stadium for our three children and their friends—a

5

monstrous mass of frayed coloring books, one-eyed Teddy Bears and bread crusts growing penicillin beneath a milk-stained daybed. I wrote in my bedroom.

The color photograph on the calendar hypnotized me—classical columns and high arches, alabaster and rose, against a painfully blue sky. *Roman Forum and View of Colosseum.*

"Italy," I said. "We will live in Italy. We will learn Italian. I will drive an Alfa-Romeo, wear a beret and sit at sidewalk cafes, discussing Silone with Moravia, or Moravia with Silone. That'll show 'em!"

David, who was two and a half at that time, climbed out of the high chair. In Doctor Dentons, his rear end was malformed and enlarged by several layers of diaper. Marie studied him.

"Find out if they have diaper service in Italy," she said.

Her indifference did not deter me. The word was spread around—we were Rome-bound. We would stay a year. Two years. Forever! I was feeling less square by the minute. How I longed to meet that actress again! I'd grab her beads, dunk them in my No-Cal and sneer: "Who's square now, blue eyes?"

But the inevitable happened. People would hear of my grand scheme, cock their heads and ask insultingly: "Why Rome?"

"Rome," a poet told me, "is tawdry."

An artist added: "Rome is dreadful—filled with Americans. Go to Positano. Or Ischia."

"If you like Hollywood, and I doubt that you do," a television journalist whispered, "you'll like Rome. I hate it myself."

An editor shrugged a tweed shoulder. "Florence, yes. Rome, no."

Finally, a highly-priced fashion model, a bloodless stork with hollow cheeks, blew Sano smoke in my eyes and delivered the *coup de grace.* "Rome," she said, "is *square.*"

6

All plans were suspended. We could not go to Rome. Square piled on square would be too much. The Christian Democrat government would fall. Ambassador Zellerbach would frown on it. But by now we were committed. Our house was up for sale. We had airplane tickets. Moreover, I had blabbed so loud and so long about our Italian trip, that I could not back out. And then, a peculiar groundswell, a surge of public opinion, solved our dilemma. At least we thought it did.

I was in Hollywood for a week, and happened to mention my impending Italian sojourn to another writer. He was an older man, a dignified type who gave off an aura of great wheels of cheese, rare Hungarian wines, and a jade collection. "Italy in the summer?" he chuckled. "There's only one place to go."

"Rome?" I asked hopefully. "Florence?"

"No, no, my boy. You'll die of the heat and the tourists. Go to the Italian Riviera. Rapallo. Santa Margherita. Portofino. Those little places are sheer paradise."

He referred me to other Hollywood people who knew the region. "We adored it," another writer said. "My wife and our daughter spent three months in Rapallo. You'll love it too."

Finally, a story editor at a studio, who had spent one night in Portofino, a persuasive, intellectual man, provided the clincher. "For a writer, it's unbeatable. Clean, inexpensive, accessible, uncrowded."

And so, my mind was made up for me. How could Rapallo fail to please us? Oh, memories of Pound and Beerbohm and the Treaty of Rapallo! I would show them all—the lady tie-dipper, the lawyer who exposed my financial stupidity, Jack Kerouac—the whole mocking army of the unsquare!

I did not gauge my own powers. I was the Typhoid Mary of

Squareness. The lush Riviera, the breath-taking rugged coast-lines, the sparkling beaches and glittering waters—all these would turn to clay beneath the tread of my 12-E Coward arch-supporters.

CHAPTER two

goodbye to
all that crabgrass

It was time to break the exciting news to our children.

We were going to a country called Italy, to a wonderful place called Rapallo, far, far from their snug little world of The Three Stooges, Nursery School and Frozen Waffles. What jolly times they would have in Rapallo!

Nancy, our oldest, was six at the time. She distrusted the project immediately. A dark, wary, observant child, she has a voice that shatters wine goblets. We have often contemplated legal action against the man who removed her tonsils. Following the surgery, Nancy's voice rose two octaves, and has never come down. (I'm joking of course about legal action. Besides, Marie claims she is not sure *who* the doctor was. In modern suburban medicine, the patient never sees the physician, but deals with nurses, receptionists, wives and internes.)

"The only way I'll go to Rapallo," Nancy shrilled, "is if Janet comes also."

Janet was her best friend. They were in perpetual conspiracy against all other little girls in Westbury—a kind of John Birch Society for six-year-olds. Their favorite gambit was to stage costume plays. Nancy and Janet always had the leads. The other little girls were awarded supporting roles— dogs, servants, furniture. According to a souvenir program I have kept of their last production of the shortened 1959 season, their last offering was called *The Royal Livers*. I took this to be a drama about Louis XIV's *pâté de foie gras* factory, until I realized that the *i* in *Livers* should be an *o*.

"I ast you if Janet could come," Nancy said, frowning.

"Maybe for a weekend," I lied. "It's up to her Mommy."

"Okay, you promised," Nancy said. Clearly, she had no use for Rapallo in advance.

Teddy, our middling child, was four at that time. He is a placid fellow, given to cool, complex thoughts that are no one's business but his own. He is the kind of child who silently nurses a grudge for years. "Once you left me in the car when you took Nancy ice-skating," he told Marie darkly one day. She had indeed—when he was a year and a half old. I had the uneasy feeling that the Italian Riviera would endow him with a decade's worth of harbored grievances.

Our youngest, David, was most easily enticed into our

10

quest for romance. His first pet, a black and white cat, had just died. Fifi had crept into the motor of our car to keep warm and—never mind. A garage mechanic assured us it had perished painlessly and quickly. We told David that his cat Fifi was lost. "No it ain't," he said. "It's dead. Nancy told me. George Washington's dead also."

"Did Nancy tell you that?" I asked.

"Yeah. My cat and George Washington is dead."

I pondered this, but made no comment.

"George Washington was a cat," he said. The child was a genius. He was dealing in syllogisms at two and a half.

I told David about Italy, and Rapallo, and the airplane ride, and added slyly: "And you can have another cat there! Italy has lots of cats!"

"Yeah," he agreed. "And George Washington."

Thus having deceived our issue, we approached D-Day.

Westbury, Long Island, had been good to us. In my innocence, I had never felt guilty about our modest red brick house, identical with 62 other red brick houses, resting amid nourished ilex and ailanthus on a former potato field. I had read all the sexy novels about suburbia, and all the sociological best-sellers about the terrors of conformity, the horrors of fresh air and P.T.A.'s and clean rooms and lawns, but somehow all this had eluded me. Now, on the verge of our European adventure, I felt sorry for Westbury, for my helpful, kind neighbors (one poor man, a manufacturer of storm windows, spent half his free time helping me assemble redwood tables, Jungle Jims and other outdoor impedimenta) and their orderly, normal lives. They had all read Vance Packard, William Whyte and assorted Jeremiahs—and they couldn't care less.

A going-away party for Marie and myself found me deep in

gloom. We were off to the Riviera—a new world of art and beauty, of the sensual and rarefied—and our friends would sit at home, catching the 7:37. Good fortune embarrasses me. I began to drink.

But as the evening progressed, it became evident that far from being *envied*, I was being *pitied*. One friend, a plastics manufacturer, set the tone, when he advised me: "I saw Europe during the war—England, Germany, France. You can keep it. One church looks like another." I suggested that 15 years might have made a difference. "You can keep it," he reiterated, dragging on his *Partagas*. "What I wanna go for? I got a freezer full of steaks, a barbecue, two cars, a boat. I can fish or play golf whenever I wanna. Who needs Europe?"

"The Europeans," I said meekly.

"See what I mean?" he shot back. "That's who belongs there. Not me."

"Yeah," a young research chemist added, with a touch of belligerence. "Who needs all that?"

"The way I feel," a realtor's wife joined in, "is who has to go tramping around ruins in the sun? You can read it in books."

"Or see it on TV," a builder added.

"What do you do about antibiotics over there?" a cosmetics jobber asked. "I understand all that stuff is strictly black market. Me, I can miss that kind of existence. Gimme my place right here in good old Nassau County."

Oh, Vance Packard! Oh, William Whyte! How you have missed the point! How you have mis-gauged, under-estimated and misinterpreted the people of the suburbs! Far from being neurotic, unsettled and anxiety-ridden, they are the world's *happiest* people! They have it made. They like their TV, their freezer, their supermarket. Europe means a lot less to them

12

than that damp spot in the basement. And they are a good deal happier than *you*, Mr. Vance Packard, and all you other fellows who worry about them so much!

The party was a great success. Everyone wished us *Bon Voyage*. They expressed concern about medical care, playmates for our children, availability of whiskey and cigars. By now I had a throbbing migraine headache, brought on by the odor of bridges burning.

I had hoped that Marie had been spared the ordeal. But she, sucker that she is, beat it down to the local pharmacy the next day and bought a gallon of aureomycin in raspberry syrup. At $75 it was a bargain, considering the peace of mind it gave her.

CHAPTER three

taking the plunge

My wife and I believe in a fair division of marital chores. We break it down this way: she does the work, and I worry for both of us.

It was therefore agreed that she would remain in Westbury, sell the house, put our earthly goods in storage, ship our trunks to Genoa, and deal with the children's imminent psychic collapse at being uprooted. All these simple tasks Marie would handle in her usual buoyant manner, while I would fly—alone, fretting, miserable—to the drab city of Paris to get our Citroen car. While she was snug and warm in Long Island, I would suffer the chills of that gray, wet place, then essay the lonesome trip down the Rhône Valley to Nice, then cross the border and continue to Rapallo, to find our villa.

I offered no objections to this unfair arrangement, since I am of a generous nature. Later, Marie claimed I had coffee-housed her into the deal. "Teddy and David ran fevers for three days," she complained, "and the guy who bought the house took advantage of your absence to browbeat me. I had to leave him the sandbox and the sliding pond before he'd sign." Her tone clearly indicated she suspected me of living the High Life in Paris with assorted international beauties.

"The nearest I came to a romantic adventure," I told her haughtily, when we had settled down to formal debate in Rapallo, "was in the lobby of the Hotel Angleterre in Avignon, where an *invertito* from Omaha made goo-goo eyes at me. I spurned his advances for a hot bath and an early bed."

As I recount this last incident, it emerges as additional evidence of my hopelessness. Had I a crumb of integrity as a writer, I would have responded to the fellow's friendliness and written a play about it.

Actually, it was a forewarning of my own capacity to nullify my environment, to fail to respond. A few days earlier, in Paris, similar red flags had been flown—warnings that my squaredom was beyond redemption, even in the gayest, most sophisticated of places.

I had been invited out to dinner by two married couples— the husbands both writers. At the restaurant, we were joined by a third couple (I was batching it, as they say). The male member of this pairing was an American millionaire, newly minted. He had harvested wagonloads of dollars through the high-pressure sale of a depilatory. If the product was somewhat sinister, his mode of advertising it was downright treacherous—

intemperate, threatening television commercials, that scared middle-aged women out of their wits. Now he was rich, independent, a friend to artists—and Europe was at his alligator-shod feet.

That night, Europe came in the shape of a 19-year-old French girl. She was a lithe, diffident beauty, with a splendidly disdainful nose and upper lip, white, white skin, and eyes as green as lime jello. There was a wonderful faintly soiled quality about her (difficult to achieve at 19, but the French—) and she had deliberately dressed *down* for the rather fancy restaurant we were at. She wore a belted raincoat, a tight powder blue suit, and a beret. Indeed, she was the kind of girl one found sauntering under stage lamp-posts in Broadway musicals of the 30's. I noted in her a certain command presence, and I admired it.

"Know what the kid does for a living?" the anti-hair king asked me.

"Student?" I asked. "The Sorbonne?"

The millionaire laughed at my naivete. Then he went on to explain that his date—her name was Aimée—was the featured performer at a night club specializing in *le strip-tease*. It was her night off.

"She don't just strip," he told me, "she has a real class act. It's like she's on the beach. And she takes it all off. Then she lays down on the sand, on her belly, reading a book. With eyeglasses."

It didn't sound like a terribly wild act to me. I confessed that a Tramp Band I had seen once at the RKO Albee in Brooklyn would have amused me more.

"Oh, I ain't come to the beauty part," he said. "She makes them jump."

16

"Them?"

"Her rear end. She reads the book, and every few seconds, her behind jumps. She can make it jump up, down and sideways."

There seemed nothing left to say. I studied Mlle. Aimée, and she rewarded me with a *gamin* grin. Soon, we were conversing in French. She really was a student, she said. She went to afternoon classes at some institute. She loved writers. She was studying English. Did I know Mr. 'Aminkway? Now and then she patted my hand. I trembled, and responded with witty anecdotes about Ralph Waldo Emerson.

Hair-remover was looking gloomier by the second. He spoke no French. By the time the awesome check came, he was irate enough not to pick it up. We all had to chip in—for writers an ultimate insult.

Drunk with my conquest, I promised Mlle. Aimée everything. I would send her autographed copies of my books; I would get her an introduction to Mickey Spillane; I would see about an honorary membership for her in the Mid-Century Book Society.

"Ah, you understand me so well, *m'sieu,*" Aimée whispered, as we strolled down the Champs Elysees. "Some day I shall give up my career. I shall live in an old stone house in Brittany, and write poems."

I was on the verge of a triumph beyond my maddest dreams. But in the long run the depilatory king prevailed, as they always do. At 3:00 AM, a migraine was nibbling at my left temple. My shoes were too tight. Moreover, while the millionaire had welshed on his offer to buy dinner, he was still ready to pick up Mlle. Aimée's share of his hotel bill at the Ritz.

She deserted me at the hotel, following his black mohair'd figure into the lobby. In the Paris night, his white-on-white tie gleamed like an Ethiop's eye. As she walked, I studied her income-producing asset, the anatomical advantage that had crowned her queen of strip. It wiggled no more than is normal in a 19-year old girl wearing a very tight skirt and high heels. I concluded that unlike me, she saved her art for the paying customers. Blabbermouth that I am, I will be witty and literate for free.

One of my writer friends watched me narrowly. "Thought you'd run off with her," he said. "That crazy Berlitz French had her going."

"Only it's too bad Sid got so sore," said the other. "He didn't pick up the check because you were so attentive."

Apologizing, I hitched my trench coat around my padded shoulders and strode off in search of a taxi. The air of weariness, of oddly triumphant defeat looked good on me.

Yet, the following morning, motoring south, I could not rationalize my failure or suppress a sense of loss—a grand chance missed forever. I thought about it all the way down the Rhône Valley—in Vienne, where I dined at La Pyramide while reading Charles Frankel's *The Case for Modern Man,* and concluded that French cooking made a pretty good case; in Avignon where Europe's surrealism first struck me as I studied the austere Palace of the Popes hard by a shabby theatre showing *Apache Guns;* and in Nice, a city suggesting Miami Beach with menopause.

All the way to the border at Menton, I thought of Mlle. Aimée and her educated buttocks. She was the soul of France— logical, industrious, stylish, practical, beautiful. She knew where the money was. It was at the Ritz, not at the third class trap in which I was bedded down on the Left Bank. Long after the Fourth Republic has been replaced by a Fifth and a Sixth, long after Algeria is pacified and independent, long after France follows us, and the Russians, underground into fallout shelters, I know that Aimée, redhead of my dreams, will be on the job—stripping, reading Kant on a spurious beach, and agitating her nether cheeks for the tourists.

On entering Italy, I learned at once the pitfalls of driving a foreign car, particularly a rare item like a Citroen. Any strange auto (odd in a country overrun with tourists) draws a smiling crowd. But the Citroen, with its original hydraulic system which adjusts itself with sighs, wheezes and downright flatulence, is a guarantee of claustrophobia. My French car supplied more happiness to the hearty Genovese than anything since the Marshall Plan. Crowds assembled to watch my strange *màcchina* rise with a sigh, then sink with a gasp. I was waved at from windows, cheered by truck drivers, applauded by street urchins. In Savona, a fascinated traffic cop made me put the car through its bag of tricks for a Sunday school outing. For a moment, I thought he was going to charge admission.

As the Citroen rose, the assembled citizens of Savona rose with it. It descended, and they lowered themselves accordingly. Shouts of joy accompanied the car's performance. *"Che bella! Che cosa meravigliosa!"* The automobile and I took more encores than Anna Moffo at La Scala. With their loud Ligurian voices ringing in my ear—*Bis! Bis!*—I sped on to Rapallo, my port of call.

It was a frigid, windy April night when I drove cautiously into the resort that was to be our home for four months. Great salty waves broke over the Lungomare—the palm-lined promenade that faced the Gulf of Rapallo. The streets were deserted, except for a half dozen boys listlessly booting a soccer ball about the piazza.

First impressions can mislead. It is my suspicion that more often than not they are accurate. And my first impression of Rapallo was that it was all wrong for us. Or, to be generous, we were all wrong for it. The trouble was, it was a resort—a rather tacky, uninspired, repetitious resort, in spite of Ezra Pound. The Lungomare was rimmed, on the land side, by a semicircle of restaurants, bars and tourist shops. Behind these, and bordering a small park, were the hotels. For the most part, they were peeling, slanted structures, resigned to another season of Germans, English and Scandinavians. Even on that cold April night, with the season barely underway, the streets lay under an ineradicable odor of fish frying in oil. In Italy, I was to learn later, and especially in crowded resorts in the summer, all odors are magnified until one loses all nasal sensitivities.

Weary, burdened with a sense of impending disaster (what would my churlish children do all summer? who would Marie talk to?) I checked into the nearest hotel, a sloping waterfront affair called the *Ideale*. My room smelled of fresh shoe polish and sewage. The former odor derived from the night porter's cubbyhole, which adjoined it; the latter from that novel Italian invention, the waterless toilet.

Despondent, I labored through a tired dinner of *fritto misto* and soggy greens, washed down with a half litre of that inferior wine labelled *Portofino*. As I gloomily force-fed myself, I became aware of a thick guttural hum rising about me, as if throats were being roughly cleared, nasal sinuses emptied. The harsh noises came from everywhere—all the diners in the *Ideale's* restaurant joining in. Then it dawned on me: they were speaking German. I was in a nest of Nordics, the heirs to Goethe, Hegel and

20

Schlegel, making the most of off-season rates in the land of their former ally.

They favored me with flat, disapproving stares, as if annoyed that I would automatically cause the cost of a night's lodging and a meal to rise. Or were they measuring me for one of those sets of striped pajamas? Was it my imagination? Am I hypersensitive? At the next table, a well-larded trio studied me unblinkingly, with the flat, hard stares I remember in photographs of Fritz Kuhn. One of the women—there were two middle-aged ladies and an elderly man—appeared to be shouting at me. This, I *know*, was my imagination. Still, I was disturbed, agitated. When I stumbled out of the dining room, my departure was accented by hearty *gemutlich* laughter.

Escape—I sought escape. And as I plunged into the lobby, I bumped into Ezra Pound. The great poet, teacher, literary innovator and broadcaster, in floppy black hat, cape, beard, sandals, was flanked by two attendant women. He swaggered by me, probably composing cantos on the run. Alone in the lobby, I felt naked, helpless. Between the disapproving Deutschlanders and the poet laureate of Fascism, I had an irrational feeling that maybe Europe didn't want me.

Cheerless, I walked out of the shabby hotel. The sea wind whistled across the Lungomare and whipped spume into my face. I paced the promenade with what I hoped was the grace of an Eric Ambler agent under pressure. I reassured myself that Europe had changed; the Germans had changed; Fascism was no more. Now that the northern conqueror was fat and sleek and content, I must be grateful. Now that Ezra Pound, poor man, is reduced to a pensioner's lonely life in Rapallo, I must rejoice.

In the half-warmth of a neon bar I sipped bitter espresso and watched the salty combers smash at the sea wall, break in foamy anger against a 13th century castle. For some reason, I kept thinking of Bremen, Germany—where I had last been stationed in Europe, and where, after repeated protests by the citizens as to their innocence, the Canadians unearthed a mass grave with 10,000 bodies!

And now I had willingly come back to Europe, dragging a suspicious wife and three mutinous children. In the gaudy splendor of the espresso palace, I drank my bitter brew alone.

CHAPTER four

the art of renting a villa

My mind was made up: I would leave Rapallo.

But I did not reckon with *La Dottoressa*—a woman I have learned to love and fear. *La Dottoressa* is a pediatrician, an Italo-American. She is the unofficial hostess for all sojourning Americans in Rapallo. I had been given her name by the aristocratic Hollywood writer, who had once lived there.

"You *must* see her," he said, "if only to give her my love. A remarkable woman—from Albany, New York—but more Italian than any Italian. Her husband is an internist. Two marvelous doctors—and marvelous people."

Everything he said was true. He neglected to mention, however, *La Dottoressa*'s persuasive powers. She is the kind of pediatrician—God bless her!—who can convince a three year old boy that a painful injection of penicillin is more fun than a Mickey Mouse cartoon.

I checked out of the *Ideale,* noting that the manager was a dead ringer for General Heinz Guderian. He barely acknowledged my request for a bill, chuckling as he was over old Afrika Corps shenanigans with two other *Tedeschi.* The Italian Riviera was a branch of I.G. Farben.

Before leaving for the south (where? why?) I called on *La Dottoressa.* She received me in her immaculate office. Vivacious, prematurely gray, pretty, she was a woman of purpose, intelligence and charm. And she utilized all these to entrap me. At once, she sensed I was a sucker for doctors. Moreover, she is dedicated to the advancement of Rapallo at the expense of the rest of Italy.

I delivered greetings from the Hollywood chap, then told her I was headed south, that Rapallo didn't seem to meet our needs.

"Nonsense!" cried *La Dottoressa,* "you haven't even looked!"

In one swift gesture, she rose from her chair and began frantically to dial real estate agents. The first three she called told her that there was nothing—absolutely nothing—available in the way of a large villa. I got up, gratified.

"Sit down!" she ordered. "It doesn't mean a thing! They all say that the first time! Besides, I have all sorts of contacts. *You will not leave!*"

The reader will recall the manner in which the beagle breeder sold me the coffin; the bargain foreign car that never ran properly; the TV AM-FM Short Wave set that is forever defective. Another inside deal was to be my undoing.

As *La Dottoressa* kept phoning, whipping the Rapallo Realty

24

Board into line, I reflected on what had so depressed me the previous night. Surely it wasn't the Germans. I knew they were defanged. It was the shock of proximity: the realities of revelation. Fodor's guide and all those Hollywood people who had enraptured me with tales of romance, had now run into the actualities; they had lost. Rapallo, I knew at once, was no place to drag three small protesting American children. I had glimpsed the beach during my stroll—a tiny crescent of blackened sand, rimmed with green lockers. By comparison, Orchard Beach in the Bronx was Deauville. (I have a hunch I have used the wrong paragon, that Deauville is pretty sleazy also). Moreover, I suffered a sense of being locked in—mountains on one side, sea on the other. The nearest airport was at Milan, 155 miles away.

Suddenly the Riviera myth infuriated me. Why must I be party to fiction? Why do the names Rapallo and Portofino connote an elusive magic? Why were the rocky, skimpy beaches preferable to the clean white sand—miles of it—at Long Beach, New York, where I had spent boyhood summers?

Wherein the grand privilege of being suffocated by the stout citizens of Munich and Frankfurt, weathering their steely laughter and gutturals, as opposed to a friendly gathering of Iowans at Santa Monica, California? Or pleasant Brooklynites at Miami Beach? And to judge from the previous night's meal, and the fish-fry odors in the street, Rapallese cooking ranked with roadside eating in South Carolina.

My reverie was shattered. "Todini has several lovely villas for you to look at!" *La Dottoressa* said. "I'd go along, but I have calls to make. Go, go—"

"But I really don't think—"

"You don't think anything of the kind," she said, shoving me out of the office, as a woman laden with the neatest twins I

25

have ever seen—one on each arm—brushed by me, "Todini is most reliable. People simply do not come to Rapallo and then just run off. Rome is insufferable. Naples is worse. You must stay here."

"Why?" I asked weakly.

"Because *I* have made up my mind," she said. "Besides, where else will you find an American pediatrician to look after your *bambini?* Make sure you tell your wife that!"

Oh! *Dottoressa!* What a low blow you struck! She had found the clincher—an American pediatrician to jab shots into their quivering bottoms, to ram suppositories and pills into them, to pacify my wife's normal suburban neuroticism. I recalled that $75 demijohn of aureomycin and ran off to my appointment with Todini.

Andrea Todini, proprietor of the *Agenzìa di Belleza* (Beautiful Agency) was standing in front of his office on a side street. His thumbs were hooked in his vest pockets. He wore a wide-brimmed black hat, the rim upturned, and eyebrows that projected an inch from his gloomy, seamed face. As I studied my benefactor, the miracle of international commerce became apparent to me. Todini's misery crossed boundaries and oceans; his misery was the misery of all real estate agents, and his first allegiance was to that world-wide brotherhood of artful dodgers. Thrust willy-nilly into the midst of Jamaica, Long Island, Todini could have skilfully held down a desk at the Acme Realty Company on Hillside Avenue. On the other hand, he would never have made the grade, as, let us say, a street-car conductor in Sicily.

As soon as he was beside me in the Citroen, he confided that what I sought was *impossible*—there was nothing to rent in Rapallo. With some pique, I pointed out that he had told *La Dottoressa* otherwise.

26

"*Signor* Gren," he said morosely, "how can I disappoint so great a lady?"

(Italians have trouble with the *ee* in *Green*. Except for those fluent in English, my name emerges as *Gren*, to rhyme with hen).

We motored into the winding dirt roads. Todini kept shaking his head negatively. "The problem is you want to rent for May and June, as well as July and August. May and June *non è stagione*."

Non è stagione—it is not the season. We were to hear these three words a hundred times during our Italian junket. It would not be the season for renting villas, for sneakers, ice-cream, lubricating cars, having babies, buying a cat—name it. Italians have simplified their lives in this manner. They apportion life's functions and needs into phases of the moon, I suspect. Try to buy a bathing suit in Italy in February.

I asked Todini why we were bothering to make the trip, if no villas were available.

"Perhaps we may find a *padrone* who is crazy enough to rent in May," he replied—hinting at my own insanity.

That day with Todini lingers in my memory as a compote of damp, malodorous rooms, flaking old ruins set on dizzying heights above the sea, sullen custodians, gardens rank with savage weeds and moulting palm trees—a nightmare of Mediterranean vistas and smells. All morning long I kept recalling a Truman Capote novel in which a character lovingly remembers a dreamy Mediterranean villa with "crumbling pink steps." Somehow those friable steps had stuck in my mind, and now I was treading them—pink, blue, saffron, mauve. Not only were they crumbling, but cracking, falling, and steep enough to induce angina pectoris. The Citroen gasped its disapproval as we drove higher and higher. We looked down from sheer drops of a thousand feet to

27

the sea rocks below; I wondered how Marie would feel with our children scampering along the cliff edge like Gibraltar's Barbary apes. I flushed halfhearted toilets, shuddered at kitchens layered with grease, and found myself shouting at Todini, who rarely answered, becoming increasingly dour as the day ground on.

In late afternoon, he had an inspiration. He had forgotten all about a certain wealthy English lady, who was reopening her villa and wanted to rent—he thought. "Very high class," Todini said. "She is fixing it right now. Of course, with kids like yours, she might not want to, especially when *non è stagione*—"

I parked the Citroen at a 40 degree angle on the dirt path leading to Lady Mildred's villa, and we entered a garden where Rapaccini's daughter once wandered amid the noxious blooms. Hideous cacti encroached on salvia and lupin; squat peeling palms slouched against ancient stone benches and waterless fountains. An obese cupid, noseless and emasculated, lurked in the rank undergrowth.

The villa—I describe it in detail because it was a prototype of the others—was painted an emetic yellow, with toxic green shutters. It had three stories, heavy cornices, and listed slightly to seaward. If one stood at the edge of the stone balustrade on the cracked patio and bent over, the main tracks of the Nice-Rome express train were visible directly below. I had a vision of our issue spilling over the rail and being mangled beneath the wheels of the trains that Mussolini made run on time.

"You'll get used to them in a day or two," Todini muttered. "Only twenty-two trains a day."

The high green doors of Lady Mildred's villa were opened. In a cavernous foyer, an Italian couple in blue work clothes were dusting. At least I *think* they were dusting. Each manipulated a long-handled raffia broom against the ceiling and upper walls.

Apparently, they were after cobwebs. What they succeeded in doing was to smear cobwebs, dust, grime and broom-straws in an irregular patina.

Todini shouted, *"Permesso! Permesso!"* in a few seconds Lady Mildred appeared.

I preface my comments with the confession that I am a hopeless Anglophile. I like the English. But in the case of Lady Mildred Raw-Haddon, my affection was strained. She was an elderly woman with Wedgwood blue eyes and a crown of white fluttery hair. Thickly built, uncorseted, she swiveled about barelegged on blue sneakers, assuring me that a bit of a wash and air, and the villa would be in "slap-up" shape.

A proper English public school accent has a built-in quality that disarms and defeats me utterly. Suddenly I am ashamed by my own harsh speech. My Brooklynized dental T's get thicker, my A's flatter, my manner menial and apologetic. If I had a forelock, I would tug at it.

An Englishman—more so, an Englishwoman—who speaks in upper class accents and a cadence, can mouth the most infamous idiocies, the most patent nonsense, the starkest misinformation, and sound eternally right and wise. Thus, when Lady Mildred informed me: "A bit of sprucing up, and the old place will be top-hole!" I believed her.

As I watched her two Italian bondsmen smearing dust, I betrayed a certain nervousness. She edged closer. "Yoah wife will love it heah!" she cried. "Close by everything—but secluded!"

As she advanced, tweed suit, sneakers and white halo, a heavy odor of strong whiskey assailed me. Lady Mildred had been at the bottle. My inability to tolerate alcohol extends to alcoholic breath. I recoiled.

"Ah—where's the furniture?" I asked. The rooms were not

only filthy, they were barren. In that damp eyrie, with Scotch vapours resting heavy on the air, not a breeze stirred.

"It's all in the kitchen, nicely stacked for the last two years. We'll set it all up after we've cleaned."

She led us to the kitchen. Stacked, they had not been. *Dumped*, they were, as if from a chute. Dismantled iron beds lay athwart unravelling old straw chairs. Broken vases and stained ashtrays littered the dirty tile floor. An antipasto of pillows, cushions and mattresses had been utilized as stuffing in the interstices between the hard goods. Six months of airing, purifying, disinfecting and painting, it seemed to me, would be needed to render that musty collection of junk approachable.

As we followed her in a dark corridor, she indicated the rent she expected. "*Per la stagione*, naturally, I expect 400,000 lire." *La stagione* again—July and August. She wanted $640 for the season. I hesitated to even mention the forbidden months of May and June.

Upstairs, it was darker, stuffier and clammier. Lady Mildred assured me that everything would dry out when the shutters were opened. Italian shutters are of slatted wood, controlled by a wide tape. They are fashioned to convert the brightest hot daylight into sable darkness, so that the citizenry can take its midday snooze comfortably, and so that all commerce and industry may be effectively halted.

We approached a bedroom. It yawned like Hell's mouth.

"Do come in with me," Lady Mildred said. "This would make a lovely nurs'ry."

She vanished in the murk, unsteady on her sneakers, like an old Wimbledon veteran. Todini and I followed her, freezing at the sound of a loud, thick *crash!*

"Oh deah," we heard her say, "I do believe I've fallen."

Terrified, I envisioned our hostess with at least a fractured pelvis, the inevitable trauma that strikes old ladies on the booze. Todini and I charged around the room. In the absolute blackness, we couldn't locate her.

"Is there a light switch?" I called anxiously.

"Oh deah me, no," Lady Mildred giggled. "The electricity isn't connected until July."

The realtor flicked his cigarette lighter. Lady Mildred rested in a disorderly heap, just to the right of the threshold.

"Be two sweet boys and help me up," she said.

Todini and I raised her slowly; he seemed singularly unmoved. "Are you all right, Lady Mildred?" I asked. "Are your legs okay?"

"Oh, I'm tip-top," she said gaily. "Just a bit of a tumble."

A bit of a tumble! She had hit the marble floor like a Grand National loser going down at Becher's Brook. That hard thud had all but shrieked: *fracture!* Yet here she was, up and sassy, padding on her Keds into the next room.

"Heah is the mah-ster bedroom, Mr. Green—"

Crash!

Once more she had sneaked into a dark room, and once more she had hit the marble. The noise this time was even louder. She must have struck the floor at a different angle. Todini and I raced after her. He had his Zippo blazing as we entered. She rested against one wall, a pile of boneless Harris tweed—laughing.

"Aren't I the silly?" she asked. "These awful, awful marble floors." She tried to make it up by herself, like Ingemar Johannson just before taking the count. She held out two flapping arms. "Be little deahs and help me."

The realtor and I raised her again. There was a blue bruise

under her left eye, and her right arm wasn't brachiating properly.

"Really, Lady Mildred," I said shakily, "you don't have to show me the rest of the house. The price *is* a little high—"

"Oh, don't be frightened by that. The price is flexible. I do so like Ameddicans, especially Ameddican writers. Do you know Mr. Spillane?"

Before I could answer, she scuttered down the hallway. Todini and I kept pace. His indifference bothered me. For an allegedly emotional people, Italians can be disturbingly dour and uninvolved. Green's Law was at work again—*the habitudes of trade are stronger than ethnic traits*. Todini was not an Italian; he was a real estate agent.

"Theah's a dahling rum heah," Lady Mildred was saying, "and you could make it a stoddy—"

She had feinted us out of position. Rounding a corner, she had ducked into an alcove out of our field of vision. This time she struck the marble in two sections—*Crash! Clunk!*

In the flickering of Todini's Zippo I saw her supine, evidently *hors de combat*. Her arms and legs described a large X on the cold gray floor. Her angelic white hair rested around her patrician face like a nimbus.

"I'm evah so embarrassed," she said lightly. "I cahn't imagine what's gotten into me today." She did not sound at all embarrassed.

We helped her to her haunches. She squatted there. "Mr. Green, be a deah chap. Theah's a bottle of whiskey in the sideboard theah. Fetch it."

At last I knew what had kept the Empire in business so long—and why eventually it had to go under. I groped my way past Todini's scowl and found a bottle of Scotch and some dusty glasses, apparently last used to toast Garibaldi's departure for

Sicily with the *Mille de Quarto*. I poured her Ladyship a stiff belt, and two smaller ones for the agent and myself.

We raised her slowly, like a barn roof.

"To Anglo-Ameddican friendship!" she sang. "Chin-chin!"

At that moment, a good thumping migraine headache seemed in order—chastisement for my mad dream of the High Life on the Italian Riviera. There, in the musty confines of Lady Mildred's villa, I saw the dream turn to nightmare.

"In the event you decide to rent," she said, "there's one little thing you should know." Todini and I guided her out and down the winding stairs. "I keep a little room for myself below, but I nevah, nevah annoy my tenants!"

Hesitating at the door, I gazed out at the shimmering southern sea, the vista of dark green leafage below. Was the awesome view recompense for the imminent peril to my children? Horrified, I envisioned Lady Mildred, boozed and boggling, squashing them to the marble floor like caterpillars, beneath her fallen heft.

"Well, ah, I think your villa is beautiful, Lady Mildred," I lied, "but it *is* a little too expensive for me."

I raced Todini to the car. The last I saw of Her Ladyship, she had tripped on the threshold. The two servants had stopped distributing dust on the walls, and were raising her gently.

La Dottoressa refused to accept my account of the day's villa hunting. "You will *not* leave," she said. "I refuse to let you go. My husband and I will have no one to talk to all summer. Something will turn up."

She had already re-checked me into the Hotel *Ideale*.

So, I lingered, immobilized. Every day I would look at houses or apartments—and discover they were too small, or too shabby, or not available until July. I became a familiar figure on the Lungomare—as pitiful as Ezra Pound. Whereas he would amble by, thinking cool thoughts about International Financiers, I would grab passers-by by the lapels and ask them if they had anything to rent.

On the fourth day of agony (why didn't I move? answer: I'm a coward) Todini accosted me in a bar where I was sipping my fifth espresso and reading an Eric Ambler story. It was the last English-language paperbound in the local bookstore. I had bought all the others; it disturbed me that he had a whole wall lined with *German* books.

"I have heard of a villa," Todini said moodily. "You can get it for May and June. Just by luck the *padrone* is here today on business. He's a *pezzo grosso*—a big shot from Milan. Some Americans rented it for July and August, but you might talk him into it—"

We sped up the highway to the Villa Frezzolini, named for its wealthy owner. The latter had not yet arrived, so Todini got the keys from the caretaker and showed me around. It was a delight. Everything was clean, new, tasteful. There was a sparkling kitchen, spotless tile bathrooms, an adorable balcony overlooking a terraced garden bright with cherry, olive and magnolia trees. Below the garden, the Gulf of Rapallo glittered.

"What do you think he'll want?" I asked.

Todini shrugged. "The people who have it for July and August are paying 400,000 lire."

This was about $640—$320 a month. It was not a bad price at all for a handsome place like the Villa Frezzolini. I had already been disabused regarding the cheapness of everything in Italy. Shrewdly, I assumed I could get it for a lot less in the off-season months of May and June. Frezzolini would welcome the chance to pick up some unforeseen money. Rapallo looked better by the minute. Worries about July and August did not enter my mind.

At four that afternoon, the *pezzo grosso* arrived, accompanied by his wife and his son. This was my first head-on encounter with those bastions of the Italian community—the *borghese*, the upper and middle classes—and it was memorable in many ways.

Frezzolini was a tall, straight-backed gent in his fifties. Gray, handsome, he shot his words out in crisp Milanese, rather like a burp gun. He wore a form-fitting blue suit and hugged an expensive leather brief case to his chest. His wife was pretty and gentle—a woman accustomed to comforts. The boy was fifteen, but was dressed like an American four year old—short shorts, a cashmere sweater. He was fawn-like and silent, and lingered close by Mama.

Frezzolini opened up with the burp gun on Todini. At once the latter cringed. With me, Todini was off-hand, downright insolent. With the rich man from Milan, he was a cowering toady.

"What gave you the idea I was willing to rent my house for May and June?" Frezzolini sputtered. "*Mi scusi, Signor* Gren, but Todini here has misinformed you."

"But he said—" Italy was closing in on me again.

"I was mistaken, true," Todini mumbled. "I did not understand *Il Dottor* Frezzolini."

(Doctor? Since when? I had been told that Frezzolini was a paper manufacturer. Too new was I in the country to realize that a high school graduate can call himself *Dottore*. A college graduate is *Professore*. A man with graduate school education is *Commendatore Professore*.)

"But you said distinctly—" I was trembling. Where to now? Where would we live? How would we eat?

Frezzolini's wife brushed back her hair. "I could not think of opening the villa. It would be too much work. Cleaning—making those beds."

Here was more Italian logic. La Signora Frezzolini, I knew damn well—and so did she—had never made a bed or cleaned a room in her life.

"I'll do it!" I cried out. "Me! I'll make the beds and sweep and scrub!" At once, I lowered myself in their eyes. No Italian of the most trivial status will admit to menial work.

"It's out of the question," Frezzolini burped. He turned his blue back on me.

"But I need the house!" I pleaded. "I must have it! My poor wife and our three homeless children are arriving in Milan in a few days! This is the only house in Rapallo!"

Frezzolini spun around. His heels seemed to click, and I fancied him in desert tans and sun helmet leading a charge on Addis Ababa. "Three little children?" he asked. "They would make a ruin of this lovely villa. We could never get it cleaned up for the Americans who have rented it for July and August."

I was shouting. "*Io*—I—me—*moi*—I personally will clean it! I'll wash it! I'll hire people. Your villa will be spotless!"

All four studied me with a curious detachment. Where was all this outgoing Italian warmth I had read about? Frezzolini and his family, and my guide Todini, were colder than those salty waves crashing over the promenade.

"Please," I whimpered, "I am an American writer. *Scrittore. Romanziere*. I am published by Longanesi in Milano, whom I am sure are friends of the distinguished *Dottore*. Please! I need your house!"

Frezzolini looked archly at his wife. She shrugged, unimpressed. On the other hand, my self-testimonial appeared to have moved him.

36

"I will discuss it with my wife," he announced. Frezzolini, wife and son, retired to the balcony. I was shaking.

"Why did you tell me this place could be rented?" I asked Todini angrily.

"*Sbagliato,*" he said. "I was mistaken."

The Frezzolinis seemed to be in great argument. At last they entered. He made the announcement like a Colonel of the Bersaglieri informing the enlisted men they had the afternoon off. "My wife and I have generously decided to let you rent our villa for May and June—even though *non è stagione.*"

I stopped myself from kissing his hand.

We all sat at the dining room table, Frezzolini at the head. There was a rehearsed, formal quality to the confrontation that irritated me. From his briefcase, the Milanese businessman extracted a lease, an agreement on breakage, several inventories, old gas and electric bills, and other documents. So reduced was I to muttering my eternal thanks to him, that the significance of the papers eluded me at the moment. Later it dawned on me: if he had no intention of renting, why had he come to Rapallo from Milan so fully prepared? Todini, that intriguer, saw the documents and nodded sagely: *All had worked out according to plan.*

"You understand, I am still opposed to opening the house for May and June," Frezzolini said firmly. "But my wife and I are kind people."

"I realize that!" I cried. "I appreciate it! Please don't change your mind!"

What madness had delivered me to these heirs to the Medici? Somehow, they had gotten advance information about me. The King of Shlemiels was on his way!

Frezzolini was getting snappier and louder by the minute. He was loving every goad, every banderilla he plunged into my broad, dumb neck. Fanlike, he spread the papers in front of him and announced to the blue waters below us:

"You may rent this villa for May and June, for 600,000 lire."

Six hundred thousand! The assassin wanted $480 a month! And the other tenants were paying $320 a month for July and August!

"I—I can't afford that," I stammered. My bowels were queasy.

"Then I cannot rent it," Frezzolini said. He nodded at his wife and his son. Why the boy had to participate in the negotiations I could not imagine. All three got up.

"Please!" I shouted. "Reconsider! You are getting only 400,000 lire from the other Americans. And that is during the season! In my country, one always pays *less* when it is not the vacation season!"

"May and June are more beautiful than July and August," *Signora* Frezzolini informed me.

"Even so," I protested, "I cannot pay 600,000 lire. I am not Mr. Hemingway. *La prego*—I beg you—think of my poor wife and my unhappy little children!"

Frezzolini and his family sat down. He stroked his aristocratic nose, and spoke. "Very well. I shall let you steal the rental from me for 500,000 lire. That is final."

Tears welled in my cowardly eyes. I turned to Todini, my brooding Virgil. "You told me yourself he's getting only 400,000 for July and August. Why must I pay more? Why? What have I done to insult Italy?"

Todini appeared unhappier than ever. "*Il Dottor* Frezzolini has kindly reduced his price 100,000 lire already. He cannot reduce it again and keep his self-respect. Five hundred thousand is not excessive for a villa of such grandeur."

"But why must I pay *more?* No one else will rent it in May and June. *Non è stagione.* In my country—"

"Ah, you have just given the reason," Frezzolini interrupted. *"Non è stagione.* It is not the season. In renting in May and June, you break the rules. You do what is not normal. You defy tradition. For this, you are required to pay *more.*"

All had been clarified. I looked up to see four half-smiling, faintly nodding heads—even the delicate son understood. I was being disciplined. I was being taught a lesson. In Italy, one does not rent out of season. And for my flouting of local custom, for spitting at tradition, I had to be punished. The summer tenants would pay $640 in season; out of season, I was required to pay $800!

Gasping for air, I needed some time to comprehend the logic that would torment me throughout my Italian stay. Frezzolini at once interpreted my hesitation as reluctance to meet his generous terms. He assembled his documents.

"Let us depart," he said to his wife. "I can waste no more time."

"I'll pay it," I said hoarsely. My budgeting of costs had been annihilated. "But it is too much."

"In this country," Frezzolini said icily, "once an agreement is reached by two honorable men, there is no further discussion. Sign this."

Shivering with gratitude, I signed—anything, everything he shoved at me, and had so thoughtfully brought to Rapallo, even though he had no intention of renting.

With lunatic abandon, I signed, hearing Todini mutter:

"You have cash with you now? *Il Dottor* Frezzolini expects a *garanzìa* on signing. In fact, you just agreed to it."

"Yes! Yes!" I cried. "Anything. I'll pay it!" From my breast pocket I yanked a thick wad of 10,000 lire notes. Each note was worth $16. "How much? How much?"

Frezzolini and his wife held a whispered summit conference. Private diplomacy frightens me; at once I was certain they were getting ready to back out of the whole deal. Again I would be houseless, adrift, with my mutinous family arriving in a matter of days.

Insanely, I shouted at them. "Here! Here! Take my money! Is 100,000 lire enough?" The wad of bills in my hand was like a boiled artichoke; I peeled leaves as fast as I could. A huge pile of orange notes rose on the table. Any minute I expected Frezzolini to take it with a croupier's rake. But he only nodded at Todini; the *pezzo grosso* did not soil his fingers with money.

Todini dutifully stacked the *gelt,* counted it, and shoved it across the table to his lord.

"There is the matter of Todini's commission," Frezzolini snapped. "He is entitled to ten per cent, or 50,000 lire. You pay half and I pay half."

The words were hardly out of his mouth when I had already riffled another 25,000 lire off, and thrust them at the agent. Gloomily, he tucked the blood money into a vest pocket. I didn't see Frezzolini give him anything.

Ritual slaughter concluded, the ceremonies assumed a jollier air. Frezzolini and spouse were smiling at me. We chatted in French. They wanted to know about my books, what I was working on now, what had brought me to Italy. They had skewered, roasted and eaten me, and were now digesting me leisurely.

Leaving, *La Signora* had bad news for me: I could move in on May 1, but unfortunately she could do nothing about having the house cleaned. I would have to clean it when I moved in, and again when I moved.

40

I was left with Todini. We walked out to the balcony and admired the view.

The realtor was in deep misery—surprising in view of the fat commission he had just earned. *"Che cosa orrìbile per far' a un' Americano,"* he mumbled. "What a horrible thing to do to an American!"

"What are you saying, Todini?"

"Oh, *Madonna Santa,* did that Milanese cheat you! Did he charge you too much! You are paying more money than anyone in Rapallo. And for a small villa. Ai, what a disgrace, a scandal. I shall be laughed at by all other realtors for letting this happen to you."

More Mediterranean logic was revealing itself. As nearly as I could figure, Todini would now be disgraced, because I, his client, had permitted myself to be so thoroughly humiliated in a commercial matter.

I sank into a patio chair, inundated in agony. What had brought me to this seacoast in Bohemia—to be gulled, whip-sawed, humiliated?

"Ah well," I said bravely, "there's nothing to be done. It's a nice clean house. Besides, I only owe him 400,000 lire now. I gave him 100,000 already."

"You are mistaken," Todini said. "You owe him 500,000."

"Goddammit!" I screamed in English. "You were a witness! I gave him a down payment of 100,000. I have a receipt!"

"Naturalmente, you gave him 100,000. But not as down payment. Only as a guarantee in case your *bambini* break things, or dirty the house. Also to pay for electricity, the telephone, water and the gardener. How does Frezzolini know you won't be calling Brooklyn every day? But don't worry—he'll return what's left."

"Breakage? Water and electricity?" I croaked. "For a lousy two months? For this I gave him $160?"

Todini scratched his projecting eyebrows. Clearly, my stupidity had ruined his day. "It's your own fault, *Signor* Gren. You threw the money at him. You did it yourself—100,000 lire! A robbery!"

"I was afraid he'd back out," I whimpered.

"Ai, what a catastrophe," the agent said. "For two months, 30,000 would have been enough for breakage and so forth. But you insisted on giving him 100,000. He would have insulted you if he gave some back. The Milanese are known for their courtesy."

I staggered up from the chair and leaned over the balcony. The view suffocated me with its beauty. Distantly I could see the funicular gliding up to Mont' Allegre. One silver sphere rose, its mate descended, both hanging in precarium above the rugged green heights. If the management could have guaranteed a broken cable on the next trip, I would have booked passage.

"Don't feel so bad," Todini said. "So, you paid too much. Too much rent, too much *garanzìa*. But you are a rich American. It doesn't matter to you. And Frezzolini is a fine gentlemen. You'll get most of it back."

My shaggy realtor did not lie. In January of 1960, when we were settled in Rome, Frezzolini—after four registered letters from me—sent me a meticulously itemized accounting for my 100,000 lire. Down to the last lira, he listed his expenses— electricity, water, telephone, breakage. And for a two months stay, it amounted to 93,000 lire. This left me 7,000 lire, or $11.20, out of the $160 I had thrown at him.

I had no urge to further embarrass him, so I never wrote to

ask why he did not submit the actual bills, instead of just listing them. One does not humiliate these Milanese.

As I look back on my tenancy at the Villa Frezzolini, all that I have just recounted seems eminently just to me. What right had I to begrudge Frezzolini and Todini their fair shares? Pigeon that I am, mark of marks, I should have expected nothing less than a quick trip to bankruptcy. Any protest on my part would have come under the heading of boorish behavior by an unmannered American.

CHAPTER five

Mavis

Marie and the children arrived on May 1. Teddy and David were feverish and Nancy was surly. The Milan airport (it bears the menacing name *Malpensa*—evil thought) is enormous, and my family was on an economy flight. This meant that the plane landed somewhere near the Swiss border, and the passengers were required to take a forced march of several miles to reach the terminal. My wife was crying when she arrived.

"Why weep?" I asked. "You've arrived safely! Sunny Italy! Your ancestral homeland!"

"I haven't slept for three days!" she wailed. "Next time *you* can stay home and sell the house and pack and comfort the kiddies—and battle all seven of the Santini brothers!"

Was it my imagination, or was the whole world being Italianated? Poor Marie had been in mortal combat with those exemplary movers and storers, *La Famiglia* Santini, while I had been locked in a struggle with Frezzolini. I spared her the details of my shrewd financial coup; I did not mention we had no place to live after June 30.

Vaguely I recall a six hour motor trip from Milan to Rapallo, the Citroen gasping and burping under its load of valises, toys, stuffed animals, feverish children and two snarling adults. (The car was immaculate when I arrived at the airport. How, in five minutes, did my children turn it into a suburban slum—graham crackers, legless dolls, plastic water pistols, liberal daubings of modelling clay and squashed crayons? How?)

At the villa, Marie collapsed on Frezzolini's double bed and slept for 16 hours. The kids, off schedule, kept drifting miserably into the bedroom for consolation. I was no help at all. They knew me to be the engineer of their misery, and would have none of me.

At 8:00 the next morning, Marie was paralyzed in bed, the children were crying in their cornflakes, and the local flies, alerted that the house was occupied, had descended in swarms. Fat and persistent, they buzzed around each small head.

When the doorbell rang, I fairly flew to answer it. Perhaps it was a process server, and we would have no choice but to go home. But the caller was a slender, short woman in her early thirties, presumably an Italian.

"Mr. Green?" she asked, in pleasantly nasal midwestern English. "I'm Mavis Fortunata. The *Dottoressa* sent me over. If you need a maid I can work till the end of June. Then I go to work for the other people who are going to be living here."

Mavis Fortunata! Oh, blessed name!

45

Rarely have I met people with whom I have fallen in love at once, without reservation, without regret. But Mavis entranced me; I loved her the second I saw her at the kitchen door; Marie loved her; the children loved her. She is a woman who—she is Mavis.

I must tell you about her. She was slender as a teen-ager, rather pretty. She wore a finger-tip green coat, a yellow cotton dress, and low-heeled shoes. Her voice was low and soft, and, as I have said, enjoyably reminiscent of Ohio or Indiana. When she spoke, she accompanied her words with helpless flutters of her hands, puzzled shrugs, perplexed liftings of her eyebrows, down-turnings of her mouth. The impression was one of uncertainty, of incompetence. But it was all fraud. It was camouflage. Behind her innocent, pale face Mavis Fortunata hid the most resource-ful, essentially intelligent, thoroughly able personality I have ever encountered. And I am not alone in this estimate; all who have known her—the Americans, that is—concur. She was our beloved Mavis—a Princess of Every-Day Miracles, a Queen of Serendipity.

Mavis was an American. She had been born in Toledo, Ohio. Both parents were natives of the little Italian village of Camogli, a few miles closer to Genoa than Rapallo. Her mother, though, held Chilean citizenship, and in the 1930's, she got into passport difficulties with the U.S. Government, and the whole family went back to Camogli. A few years later, the father died of lung cancer. The mother, with some modest savings and the insurance money, opened a drygoods store and bought a few apartments.

Throughout the war, they stayed in Camogli. Mavis, technic-ally an enemy alien, was never bothered by the native Fascists or the Germans—and a good thing for them. For a while she worked in a Genoa bank, then as a waitress, as a kindergarten teacher, as a book-keeper. (I am convinced the Genovese made a mistake not electing her mayor). When the war ended, Mavis married Enrico Fortunata, a handsome young carpenter. They had two children, and now live with Mama in one of Mama's apartments in Camogli.

To augment the family income, Mavis began working as a nursemaid for American families in the summer months. She drew the line at other nationalities. "Italians treat the help like dirt," she confided to me, "and the English never talk to you." And Mavis could never be a mere domestic; she was deep in the bosom of the family—any family lucky enough to employ her.

What was the magic she exercised over our mutinous monsters? Now that I try to explain it, I am at a loss. It *was* magic, I am sure. Children—all ages, all personalities—adored her, followed her, obeyed her. And when she was gone, they never forgot her.

Her technique was not flashy; it defies accurate description. She was of a child's world—yet above it. She was kind—and firm. She was forever helpful—but inspired self-help. Her talents were endless. Alone, of all the people who came to our villa, she could catch fireflies for David, a child with an insect fetish. On her day off, Marie and I would stumble about Frezzolini's garden, snatching insanely at fireflies, while David screamed, and never snared a single one.

"Mavis catches dem!" he would shriek. "Mavis catches dem!"

Indeed, Mavis did catch dem. She knew where to find a bakery on a back street that sold the best cookies and the gummiest raisin bread. (They never appreciated the raisin bread *I* bought them). In a back alley, she had located a dingy old building, faintly sinister, where there were pinball machines, toy soccer games, and juke boxes—a marvelous retreat for a rainy afternoon. She could make a bow and arrow out of twigs and string;

47

she could capture a green lizard with a tiny grass noose; she played the piano at parties; she could take shorthand and type, in Italian or English; she taught Teddy arithmetic; she cut off David's tantrums with a word, or a glance; she made dolls' clothes with Nancy.

Never, in the two months she was with us, did I hear her raise her voice, lose her temper, do an unkindness—and Heaven knows our rebellious threesome were hardly candidates for the All-Around Camper awards that summer. Watching Mavis with them, I would wallow in guilt over my own miserable parenthood, my failure to realize fully the role of paterfamilias.

Marginally, I note that in addition to these feats of valor, she made the beds, swept, dusted, ordered the food and kept track of our bills—with a rigid honesty—and acted as a buffer between our own innocent persons and the subtle Rapallese.

Only once was I annoyed with her—and then, it was accidental. I mentioned to her one day how sorry I was that I did not get the Villa Frezzolini for July and August also. There appeared to be nothing else available in Rapallo.

She responded with one of those odd, puzzled shrugs. "You can blame me, Mr. Green. The day I saw you walk into Todini's, I said oh-oh, he's an American, I'd better rent Frezzolini's place right away for the two families. So I gave Todini a deposit that day and grabbed it away from you. I couldn't take any chances."

I studied her narrowly, not quite pleased.

"Oh, I'm sorry I made all that trouble for you. But I was already working for them."

My admiration for her was so complete, that I could not hold it against her. One got accustomed to seeing Mavis conquer. Indeed, she had so utterly captivated the two families from Nyack, that they kept returning to Rapallo every summer (this was their fourth) just so Mavis could look after their six children!

One of the husbands was quite candid about it, when I met him later that summer. "I don't like the Riviera. And you can keep Rapallo. I'm bored stiff. But we want to go to Europe. But where can we find anyone like Mavis? We get here. Right away she takes the kids—ages from three to fifteen—and she goes off with them. Who cares where? Meanwhile, we're free for two months to do what we want—skin-dive, travel, tennis, or just drink. Don't ask me how she does it. There's nothing for kids to do here. The beach is awful, the park is small, there are no playgrounds, no English movies, no television. But that doesn't stop Mavis—there she is, roaming the streets with our six killers, taking them on the same bus rides and boat rides they've had a dozen times, stuffing raisin bread down their faces—and they love it!"

He shook his head, wondering. "If the wife and I tried to amuse them here, they'd strangle us to death. They'd be telling the analyst how we dragged them off to Europe, away from the Country Club. But Mavis—she can take 'em to the dentist here —a guy who doesn't know from Novocain—and they enjoy it."

The man who told me this was a wealthy toy manufacturer, a man of affairs, self-made, competent, a contributor to worthy charities. He golfed in the low 90's and had a good Dun & Bradstreet rating. Yet he could not control his rebellious get (anymore than we could ours) without Mavis, the magician who brought him back to Rapallo every summer.

I spoke before of her serendipity—her occult talent for stumbling upon good things. One example will suffice. On a rainy afternoon, I suggested she take Nancy, Teddy and David to the movies.

Marie objected. "There are only two movies in Rapallo," she said. "One is a sexy thing with big bosoms, and the other is a horror picture. They can't go to either."

Mavis' left hand fluttered helplessly—always a sign that she was on the verge of a conquest. "Let's try, maybe something else is playing."

Because of my own ineptness with the children, I had begun to resent her innocent confidence. "Now look here, Mavis," I said. "You know darn well there are only two theatres in Rapallo, and Mrs. Green just said you can't take them to either. You're not to take them to Genoa today because—"

She had little time for my defeatist whimperings. "No use hanging around here," she said, hustling them into raincoats and boots. (How did she get them dressed so quickly? Why didn't they squirm and complain and struggle with her? Mavis—where are you?)

Off they went, on one of those apparently aimless promenades through the rear streets and alleys of Rapallo. In the cold rain, Mavis led them, all munching raisin bread, to an empty store where an itinerant had set up a 16 mm projector and was showing old Walt Disney films in color, with scratchy Italian sound. Our three screamers, for 50 lire a head (eight cents) were diverted all afternoon. I have asked myself a hundred times: *how did she know he would be there?* Who told her? I am positive she had no foreknowledge. Mavis did not play practical jokes. She was above duplicity with us. But she had faith unbounded; if a movie she needed, a movie there would be.

Her magic was most powerful with David. Our three year old's acculturation was proving the most difficult. Under the best of circumstances he was a strong-willed, uncooperative little cuss. Now, the change of environment had intensified all that was feisty and prickly in him. Possibly his early diet has something to do with his charm. Allergic to milk, Dave was fed soybean juice for his first year—a brown, viscous liquid, which may have endowed him with his bilious view of the world. My last recollection of him, before I left for Paris, was characteristic. Marie was parked at Idlewild, in front of a frantic procession of honking taxis, as I made my goodbyes. I had wanted to take with me a flashlight, from the auto's glove compartment. Unfortunately, David wanted it also. So there I was—en route to Europe and adventure, with my three year old son locking his grubby fingers around my torch, screaming, kicking, weeping—not at Daddy's departure, but for his inalienable rights as a property owner. I left without a flashlight.

Rapallo in the spring was no help. He yowled and yammered continually, he ate grass and insects, he threw lasagna noodles at the cook, he went limp while crossing streets and rigid while getting dressed.

In despairing moments, we mulled over the possibility of smuggling him into Naples, apprenticing him to some Italian Fagin, and letting him follow a successful career as a stealer of hub-caps. Already, he had soulful black eyes, dark muddy skin, and a furtive manner. And then Mavis went to work on him. God knows what sorcery she employed, but he turned yellow in a day. He followed her meekly about the house, sweetly called her name, surrendered toys to Nancy and Teddy and generally cooed and gurgled, as if he had never been soured by soy-bean juice and mean parents.

It had been David's obsession to try to out-eat me. The fact that I was 36 years older than he was and weighed seven times as much did not discourage him; the child has guts. If we were being served saffron rice, he would squint angrily at my portion and then scream at Marie: "Daddy got a whole lot! More than me! I want more than Daddy!"

We would succumb to his tyranny. His plate would be loaded

with rice and he would waste two-thirds of it. I took as much of this as I could. "Nuts to him," I explained. "He get's a kid's portion—like Nancy and Teddy. No more eating contests with his old man."

Denied his monster servings, David would hurl himself on Frezzolini's marble floors and shriek vengeance. He would threaten to leap off the balcony, eat a lizard and sail away in a boat—all good ideas.

Then Mavis took over. She would innocently serve all the others, then spoon out a child-sized portion of mashed potatoes on his plate. As soon as his sneaky eye would start measuring it against my serving, Mavis would brainwash him.

"Oh boy, Davey, did you ever get a big portion! Wow—what a lot of potatoes! Hey Dave—I bet you can't eat all that! So much potatoes for a little boy!"

I suspect David knew he was being had. He would stare at Mavis, love lighting his dark eyes, and then he would go to work on the mashed potatoes. But never did he holler for a bigger serving than mine. He understood that there was a certain ritual involved, and that he had better get with it.

What makes me certain of this, is that on Mavis' day off, I would try the same gambit—and fall on my face. I would shovel spaghetti with tiny clams on to his plate, shouting insincerely:

"Oh boy, Dave—what a lot! You got so much!"

At once, he would see through my cheap subterfuge. "It ain't a lot," he would mutter. "You got more." Shrieks followed. "Mommy! Daddy got more!"

At the Lido—the handsomely named shabby beach club we joined—both boys would flee from my hairy lumbering form when I tried to be a pal and teach them to swim. But Mavis—who never wore a bathing suit, but modestly tucked up her cotton skirt—could get them to float, dive, backstroke, and most incredible of all, leave the water when she called.

Ah, Mavis—there is only one like you! She could mend broken crockery with the patient skill of a restorer of Etruscan pottery. Frezzolini, Frezzolini—if you but knew the ashtrays, the lamps, the vases, the assorted ceramic junk, that our children smashed, and which our beloved Mavis restored to a spurious newness with her handy tube of liquid cement! You, Frezzolini, could never be a match for our Mavis.

I am thinking of other rainy afternoons: Mavis sitting at the dining room table, painstakingly piecing together the minuscule fragments of one of Frezzolini's living room lamps. Simultaneously, she is performing good works and amusing our children. They sit in silence, fascinated, worshipful, rid of their anxieties, glad to be sharing the European adventure. Their splendid behavior is partially the result of their love for Mavis, and partially due to anesthesia. Mavis uses an Italian version of Duco called *Tacca-tutto* (glues everything) and it gives off certain deadly vapours which induce sleep, vertigo and nausea. What a happy memory! Mavis lovingly fits together the leg of an 18th Century courtier, as fragmented as a southern playwright's libido, while our three children loll about Frezzolini's cold floors in various stages of asphyxiation, like novitiates in an opium pad.

The Rapallese citizenry, notably the shopkeepers, repairmen and proprietors of amusements, lived in dread of Mavis. We poor *Americani*, fat boys with the bag of candy, were helpless in the face of their mercenary schemes. But Mavis, fluent in Genovese Italian and slangy American, was beyond them. The average Italian, for all his vaunted shrewdness, his earthy understanding, is remarkably opaque when it comes to matters of national origin. I attribute this to the youth of the country. Actually, Italy has only been in existence as a nation 100 years, and if the French hadn't pulled out of Rome in 1870 after the Franco-Prussian war, the country might still be as subdivided as the outskirts of Los Angeles. I suppose there's a good argument to be made in their favor. Nationalism has hardly proved a blessing; perhaps the Italian's confusion over allegiances and origins is more to the point than the mad scramble for flags and anthems that is bedevilling much of the world.

Once in Trieste I was stopped by a motorcycle cop for a traffic infraction. An ill-tempered fellow, he studied the Citroen and assumed I was French. *Francese!* he kept saying—even though I spoke rather good Italian with an American accent. When I showed him my U.S.A. passport, he was dumbfounded. How could an American speaking Italian be driving a French car? He hinted that perhaps the passport wasn't mine; maybe the car wasn't. I needed all the charm and irregular verbs at my command to convince him that conceivably an American *might* drive a French car, *might* know Italian. . . .

The Italian bewilderment over national origins made our Mavis the terror of local entrepreneurs. Her simple cotton dress, her uncosmeticized face, the fact that she always had a crew of American *bambini* in tow, clearly indicated she was a domestic. And her impeccable Genovese dialect marked her as an Italian. But when she spoke to the children, she was all American. This ambivalence confused them, and then frightened them. Italians live by tradition, by repetition, by expectation of the same events and circumstances. Induce change, or uncertainty, and the earth shakes. (An aside: most Italians, especially the poorer ones, live in a perpetual state of dread. The populace is like a group of Cub Scouts sitting around a fire, scaring one another out of their wits with ghost stories. Maids in the same household invariably begin the day by trying to terrify one another with tales of imminent horror. The cook will report that the End of the World is due tomorrow, and study the cleaning maid to see if she believes it—half-believing it herself. The cleaning girl will return an hour later and advise the cook that three people in the building have died of the evil eye. An American woman we knew had a terrible time getting a 20-year old maid to come to the States with her. The older maids in the neighborhood warned her "in America the houses are wood and are full of bears.")

Mavis needed no tales of terror to frighten the Rapallese shopkeepers. They saw her slender figure approaching, and they trembled. None ever cheated her. None dared try. None gave her lip. She was beyond their comprehension—not a stupid rich American, not a poor haggling Italian.

How well I recall her finest hour! It was late in August. Our Riviera sojourn was grinding to a close. Mavis was then working for the two families from Nyack now residing in Frezzolini's house. She decided to take their six variegated children for a boat trip to Sestri Levante, some miles west—a crumbly, shabby resort, with particularly bad sewage. Kind woman that she was, she volunteered to take our three, giving her a complement of nine. I went along also—as good an excuse as any to keep from working.

The eleven of us boarded the excursion boat *Stella Nova* at the Rapallo pier. It was a clear, windless day—the sky bright with a blue dye, the cypresses and pines glittering green. I was almost moved to forget the four months of toilet smells, rebellious children, my own guilt feelings.

We settled our group on a varnished wooden bench, amid a party of noisy Germans, heavy with *pesto Genovese*, belching bad wine, and awaited departure. The skipper, a sun-seared ruffian in handlebar mustache and faded dungarees approached Mavis warily, with a Henry Armetta tilt. He had the false cheeriness of one accustomed to living on the dumbness of tourists.

"How many tickets, *Signora?*" he asked Mavis.

"Two," she said.

"Two," he repeated. "You are joking." He counted heads. "There are eleven people in your party. Nine children and you and the *Signore*. That is eleven people, so you want eleven tickets."

"But the children go free," Mavis said patiently, as if explaining the rules to him. David leaped into her lap and began to kiss her. She had reduced that prickly pear to a mooning calf, an amatory fool.

"The children do *not* go free on my boat," the captain said. He turned to me. "You understand, *Signore*, I'm a poor man with my own hungry children to feed. This maid here, whatever she is, Italian or American or what, is making fun of me—"

I started digging for my wallet.

"Don't pay him, Mr. Green," Mavis said softly. "Aren't you Graziani? Your brother owns the *salumerìa* in Camogli?"

"Suppose I am?" he asked.

"Then you have no children. You aren't even married."

"Now you make a liar out of me!" he shouted. The Germans smiled their flat, wide smiles. "Please! Eleven tickets!"

Mavis cocked her head. "*I* didn't make a liar out of you. Just don't go telling the American *Signore* here about children you don't have."

"That does not alter our argument. Please purchase eleven—"

I could see Mavis circling him for the kill, as cool as Dominguin. That mustachio'd pirate had no more chance against her

56

than Clarence (Reds) Burman again Joe Louis; it was a total mismatch, something for the New York State Athletic Commission to investigate.

"Listen Graziani," she said, "last week I took the trip to Sestri Levante with two children. Remember? Those two over there."

She indicated two of the smaller fry.

"What of it?" he asked.

"You let them ride free. I only paid for my ticket. *You* made the rules. If you take the *bambini* free once, you have to take them all the time."

"*Madonna Santa!*" he cried. "I did you a favor! Two children, free—a favor. But not nine! And that one there—he's *no bambino!*" He indicated the eldest of the Nyack group, a fifteen year old heavyweight with mournful blue eyes, munching a wedge of pizza and dreaming about the Blue-Jean luncheonette back home in Rockland County.

"He's a small boy," Mavis said. "Look—take it or leave it. We'll go to Portofino instead. The rule is, children free. You can sell us two tickets."

"Eleven," he said—trembling.

"Two."

"Eleven. Two full price. Nine half-price as a special favor."

"No, two tickets is all. What's the difference? The boat's almost empty anyway. You have to go to Sestri Levante. It'll look good for business, all these nice American kids on board."

"I won't start the boat," he said plaintively. "You must pay me. Two tickets. Nine half-fare."

"Oh, you'll start it," she said. "I promised my children a ride."

This gave him pause. He mopped his mahogany face, digesting the logic. "No. No. Two kids, okay. Not nine."

"But that isn't fair," Mavis said, raising her voice slightly. *"Non è giusto."*

"What is not fair?" he asked, edging away.

"You're not fair to these children," she said. "You say you'll take only two of them free. What am I supposed to do? Leave the other seven at home, because you're so mean?"

"Che ha detto—what did you say?" He was stammering.

"You heard me. What am I supposed to do? Leave the other seven at home?"

A sour confusion clouded the skipper's face. Mavis' mastery of Italian logic had crushed him. Her marvelous irrelevancy had settled the dispute. I have long tried to analyze her victory, and I have found a kind of twisted sense to it. Two children rode free once. Thus, a precedent, a tradition—powerful forces in Italy. The woman who negotiated this concordat now brings nine children. Ergo, nine children must ride free. But no! Nine is too much! It is unfair! Ah, perhaps it is. But what is she to do? *Leave the other seven at home?*

As totally defeated as Badoglio at Bengasi, the pirate shuffled away, even forgetting our two adult fares. I ran after him, forcing lire into his calloused palm.

"Please," I said. *"Due biglietti*—two tickets, full fare."

"That woman," he said coldly. "She cannot be your wife. She does not act like an *Americana.* She is too *furba*—cunning."

"She is a most unusual woman," I said.

"Ah, *mi scusi.* Then she is your wife."

"No. My wife is not *furba* at all."

"Then who is she?" he persisted. "I have seen her around all summer."

"She is the mother of those nine children. From the little one in her lap, to the great big one eating pizza."

The boat got underway, swimming across the turquoise waters, skirting the rocky slope. "Oh, now I see," he said. "It is no wonder she could not leave the other seven at home by themselves."

It was a rare and touching moment. What Italian can resist a rush of sentiment at the spectacle of mother love? For three centuries all that the Sienese could paint were Madonnas and Holy Children. The pirate had been done in by a national trait—and by the brilliant tactics of our Mavis.

Did I suggest her as Mayor of Genoa? Prime Minister of the whole country might be a better post for her endless skills.

CHAPTER Six

the Mother Superior
and the Siamese cat

Inevitably, it was Mavis who got David his Italian cat.

She did not get him George Washington, but that was only because we didn't ask her. Had Marie or I hinted that we wanted him as a dinner guest, I am positive we would have awakened one day to find a tall, periwigged gentleman in blue knee britches and white weskit, striding through Frezzolini's olive grove.

The new cat was one of many propitiary gestures toward our increasingly fractious children. They did not like Rapallo. They were hostile to Portofino. They rejected Santa Margherita. They refused to relate to Camogli, Sestri Levante, or a dozen other Riviera beauty spots we kept dragging them to in our wheezing Citroen. Goodness knows we tried. We simply ran out of towns.

Italians, whom I rather envy in this respect, have taught their young to live on love instead of diversion. An Italian child will go to a park and just sit or stand or walk, and get kissed every few minutes. Sometimes he will kick a rubber ball or ride a bike. There are virtually no playgrounds in Italy, and the children don't object.

Your American child (mine, for sure) demands a glut of amusement, excitement, distraction, all of his waking hours. Take our daughter Nancy. At the age of three, she was known to watch television, blow bubble gum, stroke a puppy, eat cornflakes, make cutouts and get peevish with me—at the same time.

And now we had settled in a place where there was *nothing* to do. *Nothing*. In May and most of June it was still too cold to swim. (I'll get to those Riviera beaches later—hot, foot-deforming rocks, sand blackened with centuries of dirt, about three square feet per person.) There were donkey carts in town and a small park where we helped the poor lady who rented bicycles rise into the middle class through our frequent hire of her museum collection of bikes. The old lady—we called her *La Bicycletta*—also ran a small souvenir and refreshment stand, the main feature of which was a gumball machine. I suspect we spent about 50,000 lire—$80—on that blasted machine in four mouths. For ten lire, you got a colored gumball and a colored card. The cards were fascinating. They purported to supply in formation about the various nations of the world. They were great reading—further evidence of Italy's surrealist view of the rest of the world. Herewith the card on Israel, translated:

61

ISRAEL: population, 250,000
PRODUCTS: wheat, turpentine, beans, gypsum
GOVERNMENT: monarchy
RELIGION: Lutheran

It pleased me, too, to learn from the cards, that Hawaii and Alaska were independent nations governed by 'parliamentary republics'; that the religion of Sweden was Roman Catholic; and the population of India was 'over 1,000,000.' Such instruction, I felt, was well worth the thousands of lire we shoved into the machine daily to purchase a few minutes of peace.

The boys were too young for school. Nancy needed school. We tried sending her to an Ursuline convent, advising the Mother that she was not of their faith, and would skip religious instruction, if that was all right. The Mother agreed; Italians are pleasantly liberal in religious matters.

Nancy lasted two days. Interrogating her, I hoped that her departure was not due to any theological disputes.

"Why don't you want to go back to school?" I asked. "Were the nuns mean to you?"

"Nope. They're okay."

"Was it too hard for you?"

"Nope."

"Then tell me—why did you quit?"

She frowned. "The nuns kept petting me under the chin and calling me Kay Bellow. That isn't my name."

Patiently, I explained they were being kind to her. They were saying *Che Bella!*—How pretty! But Nancy could not be convinced to return. After all, Janet wasn't in the school.

Besides—what fun it was to stay at the Villa Frezzolini all day, strangling Mommy and Daddy! Reminding them, with a twist of the knife, how nice everything had been in Westbury! And what monsters we were to take her away from all this happiness! The trouble was, she was right.

The boys complained less, but behaved worse. They decorated Frezzolini's balcony with crayons and dismembered his daisy bushes. A jar of Desitin was liberally smeared on the mahogany panelling in their bedroom. And they waged guerrilla warfare against Assunta, the fat cook whom Mavis had hired for us, an independent soul who ordered special steaks and name brand wine for herself, while stuffing us with pasta. (Superb pasta, I must admit).

Thus entombed in indolence, ennui and bad tempers, all five of us ate ourselves into neurotic obesity. I still must overcome a feeling of bloatedness when I recall those lavish midday meals with which Assunta burdened us. There would be a lasagna with *pesto* (a delectable green sauce made of crushed fresh basil, parsley, garlic and butter) tiny fried shrimp and squid, mixed green salad, wedges of honest Pecorino cheese, fresh wild strawberries in Marsala—all lavishly decorated with flies. We became fat, lethargic and somnolent, slouched at Frezzolini's table, feeding ourselves, pausing only to snarl at one another.

Without Mavis, we would have surrendered and come home, whipped—and missed the grandeur of Rome that followed our Riviera disaster. But Mavis saved us. With no great effort, she diluted the mass uprising of the children, kept them from the brink of violence, and amused them sufficiently so that Marie and I were able to do some fruitful touring that summer.

One May morning, breakfast had been its usual face-cramming affair. The main course (as always) was a Genovese bread called *focaccia*—a round, salted, oiled roll, rather tasty, about the consistency of good flannel. (The highly prized Roman

63

Christmas cake, *panettone,* is like cheap flannel.) After a few *focaccia,* two cups of black coffee, and a cigar, I was ready for my morning argument with the children.

"Listen," I said, "if you're so bored, go upstairs and start writing a book. Look at the Abbe children. Did they strangle their parents and tell them they were mean? They did not. They sat down and earned money."

Teddy and David, unhearing, began to wrestle. By now, they had learned how to take falls on the marble floors. We didn't stop them unless we heard the distinct *crack* of a breaking bone. Nancy began demanding that we fly Janet over for the summer.

Bored, I wandered into the kitchen and began to swat flies. This pastime infuriated Assunta, the cook. She liked flies. She kept the kitchen door open wide and invited them in to share her goodies. A Schweitzer of Rapallo, she. It is my theory that Italian cooks are convinced that flies add flavor to food. Or that if flies are attracted to it, it must be good.

As I engaged in my lunatic ballet, often killing three in one move—one with my forehand, one with my backhand, one on the recovery—she would scowl and mutter curses in a dialect that eluded me. (Parenthetical note on Italian flies: they have no early foot and a low speed rating, but look out for their staying power. It is easy enough to knock them down, but they will often rise from a good smack and head for the strawberries, spunky as ever. Be prepared to follow up all assumed kills.)

So there we sat—living the grand life on the Italian Riviera! Wow! Wasn't I some punkins! An American writer in Rapallo! With Portofino next door!

On the dust jacket of my book *The Lotus Eaters,* there appeared a photograph of the five of us on Frezzolini's balcony. It is a study in happiness, success, good fortune. Marie and I are smiling. The children are neat, clean, healthy. Behind us is the shimmering gulf, the green hills. It is too good. I am convinced that some of the bad notices *The Lotus Eaters* received were a result of that cursed photograph. Reviewers are only human; and humans are notoriously jealous; and it just seemed too much good luck for one man—that happy, happy family in Rapallo, magic name. *If only they knew!*

As she did on so many days, Mavis rescued us that morning. She had already made the beds, dusted and swept, bawled out the laundress for using too much bleach, caught the cook padding a bill, and showed Frezzolini's gardener how to trim the daisy bushes in such a way that the landlord would never know our boys had ravaged them.

"This would be a good day to get Davey his cat," Mavis said.

All combat ceased. All heartbreak ended. All anger evanesced. Beloved Mavis; she had the gift. And knowing her as I did, she would make the search for a cat an all-day expedition, leaving Marie and myself eight free hours to despair of my folly.

That evening, Mavis and the children returned with the cat. She had found it in a milk store, the last of a litter. It was a half-grown female Siamese, a lovely seal point with the conventional bent tail, blue eyes and screwball disposition.

"The lady in the store wanted 4,000 lire," Mavis said. "But I—"

"Got it for nothing," I said.

"If I had more time I could have. But Davey was so excited, I paid 2,000 lire. Okay?"

The price—$3.20—seemed cheap enough for a pure-bred Siamese. Mavis, however, felt she had been overcharged. She brooded about it a little.

The cat was named Fifi, in memory of its predecessor. She

proved to be our second overseas triumph, after Mavis. David all but married the animal. He was inseparable from it. He slept with it, ate with it—feeding it bits of linguini as it sat beside him at the table—and lugged it around like a prized bag of agates. When he bathed, Fifi, who returned his love, squatted on the edge of the bathtub.

Fifi was our first experience with Siamese cats. I had heard much about their intelligence, their subtle personalities, their eccentricities. But I suspect Fifi was the first Siamese cat to housebreak a child.

David, as part of our children's plot to discredit our Riviera dream, had reneged on his toilet training. It saddened us, because the little fellow had learned to use the plumbing at an early age. Now, in furious opposition to Rapallo, he reverted to babyhood. We argued with him, pleaded with him, reviewed the facts of the case—to no avail. Not even Mavis could stop his regression. We had just celebrated his third birthday and it seemed an un-fair occasion to shove him back into diapers. I suggested to Marie we let him run around naked, but she vetoed this. Again, I felt it was all my fault.

Then, about two weeks after we had acquired Fifi, Mavis had an encouraging report. "I think Davey is toilet-trained again," she said. "Three days in a row now—he's been clean."

We were delighted. Here at last was evidence that our chicks were becoming acculturated. But Mavis had a bothersome foot-note. "I can't figure it out. Maybe he's just constipated. I never see him go to the bathroom either."

"He can't be constipated," I said. "No one is in Italy. Our foods are chock-full of healthful bacteria."

"Then I'm not sure what he's doing," Mavis said. "All I know is his pants are clean and he never goes to the bathroom."

I tried spying on him, but he is a cagey child. One afternoon, I was resting my neuroses on Frezzolini's balcony, when I saw David sneak into the garden below. Fifi was at his side. Every now and then, unable to resist her, he would gather her up and nibble her dark brown ears. Suddenly he dropped the cat, and almost as quickly dropped his pants and underpants. Then he dug a small hole in the earth, squatted, performed the final digestive act, and scratched earth over it. The cat watched him approvingly. He then dressed himself and strolled off with his love.

I blinked my eyes, then sped down to the garden and confronted him. "David," I said, "people don't do that."

"Fifi does it."

"Fifi is a cat. You are a boy."

"But Fifi is my best friend. She showed me."

"But people aren't cats."

"George Washington was a cat."

Nothing was to be gained by pursuing *that* old chestnut, so I dropped the subject. A little night soil wouldn't hurt Frezzolini's garden. Lewis Mumford is all for that kind of agriculture, so why shouldn't I be? But when I told Marie of my discovery, she was shocked. "We've failed as parents," she said. "A Siamese kitten has more influence on our child than we have."

"Well, it's an improvement over what he was doing," I rationalized. "And what a sneak! Even Mavis never caught him!"

We worried about David for a few days. Every now and then I'd catch him scratching earth. And then the solution dawned on me. With a guile that still arouses pride in my breast, I simply reversed the process. Siamese, I had been told, were extremely intelligent. I trained Fifi to use the toilet. In a week, David was imitating her. It was a touching scene—the two of them side by side.

For all her good deeds, Fifi had a short, turbulent life. Something there is in Siamese cats that invites pain and conflict. One day Mavis came in carrying Fifi with a disturbing report.

"Some fat man tried to steal her," she said, in her Ohio accent. "I told him off. He said it was his mother's, but I straightened him out."

A few days later, while I was reading in the living room, a fearful growling aroused me. (Siamese can growl, squeal, murmur, and make a noise like a dentist's drill). I raced out to the private road that wound behind the villa. Mavis' fat man was back. He was walking off with Fifi, and his right arm was bleeding from a healthy scratch. He did not run, in the accepted manner of thieves, but strolled leisurely, stroking the prize.

"Halt!" I cried. "You are taking my cat!"

Fat Stuff turned and grinned. When in doubt, Italians grin. *"Mi scusi, Signore,* but it is not your cat. It is the mother's."

"Whose mother? Yours?"

"No, no. *La Madre Superiore*—the Mother Superior—at the hospital."

At the end of the private road was a small convalescent home run by nuns. He told me he was the janitor, and that he had heard about the rich Americans, and the Siamese cat and—

"One moment," I said firmly. "It is true I am an American. But I am not rich. Moreover, I am a friend to the Italian people, and I respect your church. But that is my Siamese cat. The maid who works for me bought it in a milk store in Rapallo for 2,000 lire."

"You admit it is a Siamese cat?" he asked.

"Yes."

68

"That proves it is the Mother Superior's cat. Her cat was a Siamese and it was stolen. It is impossible for there to be two Siamese cats on this little road. Your maid is lying. They all lie, especially to Americans, who will believe anything."

"She *is* an American."

"Then your children took the cat, an error."

All this time we were strolling toward the high iron gates of the hospital. So anxious was I not to be a poor ambassador that I had let him keep the cat. Fifi was growling, looking at me indignantly, as if to say—this is my reward for toilet-training David?

The fat thief rang a bell. A tall, austere fellow in the long gray coat of a concierge appeared. Crossed keys glittered in his lapels. He had the same cold eye and burp-gun speech with which Frezzolini had cowed me.

"Ah!" Crossed Keys shouted. "The Mother's cat! I knew those Americans stole it. Give it here!"

"I beg your pardon," I said. "That is my cat. My maid purchased it for 2,000 lire in a milk store—"

"She stole him. Fire her at once."

"She does not steal."

"Then the owner of the milk store stole him." He addressed the fat man. "Massimo, bring it in here. The Mother will be pleased to have the cat back. She has been in tears since it was stolen."

"Listen to me," I said firmly. "The lady in the milk store had a Mama cat which had a litter. This was the last of the litter. It is a kitten, as you can see. As much as I respect the Mother, this is not her cat. I clearly heard you say *him* in speaking of the cat. This is a female cat. *Fémmina*."

The concierge ignored me. "You are not very *gentile*. To steal a Mother's cat—"

"I am not *gentile* at all," I responded, "but I believe in everyone's right to worship as he sees fit, and to own Siamese cats."

Italian logic, I had learned, was a two-way street. I dislodged Fifi from the fat man's arms and walked away. Parting, I turned and shook a finger at them. "Please do not come back for the cat. I shall inform the Carabinieri and the National Tourist Office that you are being rude to Americans. My cat is not included in the Marshall Plan."

(On reflection, this last *riposte* sounded better in Italian: *La mia gatta non è inclusa nel Marshall Plan.*)

For two days, all was calm at the villa. Fifi stayed with David —in bed, at the table, in the bathroom. Then, one evening— during the 5:30–7:30 period which Marie called The Hour of Charm—the doorbell rang.

Mavis answered it, and as I heard her calm voice say: *"Buona sera, Madre,"* I knew that L'Affaire Fifi had not ended. I ran to the foyer to see a short, elderly nun, wearing rimless glasses and a tolerant smile.

"Good evening, *Madre*," I said. "Do you desire a charitable contribution for the hospital?"

"Oh no, *Signore*. I want my cat. The Siamese cat which your children or your maid mistakenly took from me."

At that moment, Fifi and David, united in a conglomerate ball, rolled into the foyer.

"Eccolo! There he is!" the nun cried. "My beloved Giorgio!" She clasped her gnarled hands in gratitude and called on the Virgin of Mont' Allegre.

I picked up Fifi—perhaps for the last time. Another surrender to Italy was in the making. Behind the Mother, on the porch, I could see two younger nuns—a mobile reserve.

"Madre," I said patiently. "You called the cat Giorgio. You said *he.* But this is a lady cat. I bought it in a milk store—"

Her face grew grave. All of wronged Italy stared at me from behind those rimless spectacles. *"Fémmina?"* she asked. *"Non è maschio?"*

"I swear it."

"Veramente—truly?"

"Truly." Our conversation had now assumed a splendid Hemingway quality, and I awaited her next comment. Perhaps the earth would move.

"But how can you be certain?" she asked. "With cats—"

Deftly, I upended Fifi and began probing her soft underbelly. "I am a doctor's son," I said. "One must look for—"

"No, no!" cried the Mother Superior. "That is not delicate! We are not permitted to do so—in your presence! I believe you. Besides as I look at this cat it appears much smaller than mine. Giorgio was a full grown cat."

But she had not quite surrendered. She seized Fifi's tail.

"Does it have a short tail? Like Giorgio?" She stopped in mid-tail. "Ah, no. The tail is too long. I am sorry to have disturbed you."

She blessed me, blessed our house. I gave her some money for the poor. She left, and at last Fifi was safe. Neither the fat man nor Crossed Keys ever bothered us again.

At the end of June, when our occupancy at Villa Frezzolini was ending—and, unknowingly we were headed for a nightmare of bad odors and raw nerves in July and August—Fifi died. She went out bravely, after choking on some alien substance—a garden slug, a rag soaked with furniture polish—who knows. She died in the local vet's arms. We were all miserable; we all cried.

"My cat is dead?" asked David.

"She is, Dave. Like the other Fifi."

"Like George Washington."

"That's right, son."

The kid was a trouper. At three, he had more guts than I had at 36, when I first saw Rapallo by night.

A few days later I was prowling the back alleys in search of a plumber. In Italy, one must beard the plumber amid his plungers and snakes, get a half nelson on him, and wrestle him to one's house. While it is true that their plumbers are paid about one-tenth (literally) what American hydraulic engineers are paid, they are hard men to find. An American woman I knew, spending the summer in a villa near Rome, a seaside resort where nothing worked, used to rouse the plumber from sleep at two in the morning—the only time she was sure to get him. In any event, my quarry was not in his shop and I reconciled myself to a few more days of reluctant toilets and back-up sinks.

Then I noticed my friend, the Mother Superior. We greeted one another and she asked about my cat.

"I have a sad story, *Madre*," I said. "My cat died of eating something bad. We are all very sad."

Her wise old face absorbed this. Then she pointed a waxen finger at me. "So you see, *Signor* Gren. I was right. *It really was my cat.*"

"No, no, *Madre*. You must believe me. See—that milk store across the street—where it says Yomo Yogurt. My maid bought it there—"

Her eyes were locked in awesome contemplation of the un-fathomable mysteries of Heaven. "Ah, it is so plain, *Signore!* The Lord above—*Il Signore*—He who knows all—He took poor Giorgie from you because he was not happy!"

"Fifi. She."

"I know this is hard for you to understand, *Signor* Gren. But I am older. I am wiser. You are not a bad man and you, or your maid, or your children did not mean to take my cat. But poor Giorgio's death proves it was my cat all the time."

She left me, her black robes billowing, her pious figure making a mockery of my protests.

Generously, I permitted her her naive faith. Her Giorgio was my Fifi, and she knew it. Or did she?

One of these days I shall look up a reliable medium who specializes in departed pets—there *must* be one in Fairfield County. We will stage a small séance and settle the issue once and for all.

CHAPTER seven

on the banks of
the Che Puzza

June drew to a close, and so did our tenancy at Villa Frezzolini. Now both the house and Mavis, our savior, would be transferred to ten people from Nyack. Marie and I discussed our future.

"I thought of a marvelous place we could go for July and August," my wife said. "We can get a large, cool house there, with good plumbing and a big modern kitchen. We'll be fifteen minutes from white sand beaches. There are dozens of free tennis courts nearby. I've heard the food is good. And it's only 45 minutes from a big city with lots of museums, shows and concerts. Lots of the people speak English and there's always something for the kids to do."

"Rome?" I asked. "Too hot."

"Westbury, Long Island. Ideal summer temperature."

"We sold our house."

"Maybe we can buy it back. Or rent. Look, writer, you've done the Europe bit. You've got an edge on all our tourist friends, all the professional Europe-lovers. You actually lived in Italy. Not in Rome—but on the Riviera! Rapallo! Portofino! You sat in a sidewalk cafe and stared at Ezra Pound. You made a pilgrimage to Sir Max's house. Now let that actress dip your tie in her drink!"

I was uneasy. "We've missed something," I protested. "We've spent two months killing flies, shanghai-ing plumbers and electricians, and placating three howling kids. I'm entitled to more than that. I owe it to my publisher."

Fodor's 1959 guide to Italy lay on the coffee table. I picked it up and read aloud. "Madly *chi-chi*, alluring, gay, snobbish and vibrant with something, a mood that can't be defined but certainly can be felt. Be careful; it gets in your blood. The effect on foreigners, and even on Italians from other parts is often devastating—it's impossible not to go native, and once you've done that you'll never be the same."

"Fodor didn't live here for two months with three small children," Marie said.

"That's beside the point. What is wrong with us? Why do we miss everything? *Chi-chi, alluring, gay, snobbish*. All I see in Rapallo are the fat *borghese* walking up and down the promenade staring at each other. Or their teen-age kids swarming around a juke box singing 'Hanga Downa You Haid Tomma

75

Duli'. I can get that in Coney Island. An Italian's idea of a vacation is to eat and sleep twice as much as he normally does. They go on vacation to wear dark suits, stiff collars and ties. I don't begrudge them this, but why must I witness it? Is it worth all that money Frezzolini took from me?"

"Rapallo was your idea," she said coldly.

"Europe was my idea. Italy. I'll take the rap for the whole country, not for a city of 19,000."

She brought up our immediate problem. In ten days we were without a place to live. What to do? Travel? Find another place in Rapallo? Go south to the Amalfi area below Naples? (Sometimes I am clairvoyant: in my mind's eye I saw those quaint villages of the south—Positano, Amalfi—as carbons of the Riviera: small, crowded, overpriced. A year later we toured there. I was right).

We were paralyzed. There had been a failure of nerve. "Okay," I said, "we'll blow it. We'll go back to the States like whipped dogs and buy a split-level house in Hicksville and be guinea pigs for Vance Packard and all those other wiseguys. Why can't I be like James Jones and Irwin Shaw and Bill Styron? They love Europe. They prosper here."

As we sat moodily in Frezzolini's cool living room, Nancy shuffled in—angry. The poor child's pipe-stem legs looked like connect-the-dots games. Rapallo's mosquitoes and bed bugs had dined well on her.

"I got nothing to do," she said. "I had nothing to do yesterday. Or the day before. The beach is cold and the water's cataminated."

"Mavis will take you for a nice bus ride to Genoa," I said. Sneaky Daddy! What would they do in Genoa? Or Sestri Levante? Or Milan? I longed for the warm, comforting glow of an American television set, where my issue could sit in stupor watching hour after hour of murders and inanities. My children were suffering a loss.

"We went to Genoa three days ago," Nancy said. "I wanna go home."

It seemed the only thing left to do. I reached for the telephone book. "All right," I said, "you both win. Home it is. I'll see if American Express in Genoa can squeeze us on a boat. We shouldn't have too much trouble this time of year."

As I began dialing, *La Dottoressa* entered—bouncy, gay, bursting with good news and propaganda about Rapallo. "Gerald and Marie!" she cried. "I have found you an adorable apartment! Just outside of town in a brand new building! It's a bit back in the hills—but it's gorgeous! I made a down payment for you!"

We stayed in Rapallo for two more months.

Our new quarters were the ground floor of an immaculate new white plaster building. It was a four story apartment house, each floor leading to a smart terrazzo balcony, faced with glittering mosaic. Hard by, a clear babbling brook ran into the Gulf of Rapallo, and all around rose green terraced hills studded with olive and fig trees. It seemed heavenly.

That is, it seemed heavenly from a quarter of a mile away, as we bounced up a narrow dirt road. Unfortunately, like much of Italy's beauty, it was long-range allure. Proximity broke the spell. The building was so new it was unfinished. Whereas toilets worked with a grumbling reluctance at Frezzolini's, at Casa Stoppani they did not work at all. Nor could any plumber make them work. It had something to do with the slope of the hills surrounding us. "Keep a pitcher in the bathroom," the landlord said. "It's even cleaner that way."

77

All electrical fixtures and outlets were unfastened. They just seemed to dangle out of irregular gouges in the plaster. This is apparently an insoluble mystery to Italian building contractors—the firm fastening of chandeliers, outlets, etc. I have been in the villas of extremely wealthy persons in Rome, where an antique Bohemian glass chandelier will be supported only by its nude wiring, issuant from a rough crater in the ceiling. Why?

Actually we had rented two apartments. The kitchen, living-dining room and maid's quarters were up front. We were then separated by a corridor; the second apartment, at the rear of the house contained our sleeping quarters. The rooms were small, noisy and wide open. (Screens are virtually unknown in Italy. This seems a good project for the Peace Corps).

At Frezzolini's, we had only the flies. But at Casa Stoppani, we had flies, mosquitoes, gnats, and other winged vermin—squadrons of them. The garden consisted of a few ferns and cacti, and lots of voracious snails. David began collecting them at once. They were a peculiarly slimy species—*Lumachi*, the Italians call them—and the sensation of treading on one at 3:00 am, barefoot, en route to the bathroom, and hearing the shell crack and feeling the ooze ooze cannot be listed among life's great pleasures. Occasionally, David, a wildlife expert, would adorn his growing snail collection with an evil long black slug. For a while I tried to make an asset of his zoo by regaling the boys with funny stories about Sidney Snail and Seymour Slug—but Teddy and David gauged the insincerity in my narration and got bored.

The road that twisted up to the Casa Stoppani was barely wide enough for a Fiat 600. Our Citroen, a modestly sized car by American standards, had to walk a tightrope to keep from pitching itself into the nearby stream.

78

Ah, the stream! It's true name was the *Torrente Tuscana,* and how it had glistened and gurgled that first day when we saw it from a distance! And how it smelled and sickened us up close! The local residents referred to it not by its official name, but as the *Che Puzza*—the What-A-Stink River. It did. The citizenry regarded it as an ideal depository for garbage. Wherever the *Che Puzza* River curved or bent, great heaps of refuse, garnished with flies, would assemble.

It was a fine place to conclude our Riviera dream. So far I have mentioned only the environmental charms of Casa Stoppani. Our fellow tenants are worthy of mention. They were disaster prone, and we soon caught the infection.

On our very first day of residence, I almost ended up at the bottom of the *Che Puzza* River. I was frantically trying to turn the Citroen around in a muddy clearing below the house. The car made a sudden lurch—I had succeeded in getting a front wheel over the precipice. Another foot and I would have slid down the steep bank to the What-A-Stink, amid old Chianti bottles, orange peelings, and olive pits. I was rescued by a fellow tenant, a certain Angelo Lentini, a Rapallese policeman (more on this customer later). Lentini, on his way to work, helped me wedge the Citroen off the cliff with a two-by-four, so we cheated the fetid stream.

However, to make up for matters, David, Teddy and Marie *all* fell into the foul waters that evening. I'm reluctant to recall the circumstances. Vaguely I seem to remember the boys relieving themselves (in the manner of Italian kids) Teddy tripping over David, both slithering down the embankment, Marie stumbling on them trying to save them, and all three descending to the Styx below. Aaaagh.

As I said, disaster lurked about the place. The second night we were at Casa Stoppani, we were awakened by a fearful pounding on our door, and screaming emanating from an upper apartment. I raced from our bed and opened the door to find Officer Lentini, shouting: *"Fuoco! Fuoco!*—Fire! Fire!" I yelled at Marie to grab my manuscript and the children, in that order, and to make for the hills. However, Lentini explained that the fire was luckily confined to the top story and that it was only a television set that was burning. As we flew up the stairs, Lentini apologized for awakening me, but knowing I was an American *Professore,* he assumed I knew all about television.

The owners of the burning TV were a middle-aged couple, parents of the Dottor Stoppani (a jeweler) from whom I had rented the apartment. When Lentini and I got there—he with his pad and pencil out, the essence of Italian officialdom—the television was still burning merrily. The woman was shrieking and waving her arms. The man, in pajamas, was studying the blaze thoughtfully. He looked at us sadly. "No insurance. We'll never have another."

There was nothing funny about his misery. TV sets are outrageously expensive, in keeping with the notions of commerce in Italy—small output, very high price, enormous markup, a tiny restricted market. The poor man was being victimized, and I could understand the paralysis of the collective will. Bravely, I yanked the plug out, hoping that the entire building would not short. (It did. We lived in darkness for three days.). Then I calmly walked into the kitchen, filled a glass with tap water and tossed it into the TV set's flaming innards. It hissed, smoked and died.

"Bravo!" cried Lentini. "I knew the *Professore Americano* understood all about television!" He scribbled furiously.

The woman still screamed; the man shook his head. Other

tenants poked their curious heads through the door. There was a dull hum of admiration for me. *Bravo! Che intelligente, quest' Americano!*

Blushing, I walked out, hopeful that I had done my bit in restoring some of the reputation for technology we had lost after Sputnik.

"It's their own fault," Lentini sneered as he accompanied me. "Trying to show off with their TV. Would they ever invite me or my wife to watch?"

But then, he was a Calabrese—and they are notoriously short on sympathy.

This propensity for disaster extended to the other family in the house, a strange threesome who lived on the third floor, between the show-off TV owners and Officer Angelo Lentini. I never learned their names. The family consisted of a middle-aged woman, her delicious daughter, in her early twenties, and a little girl of six. As nearly as I could make out, the little girl was the older woman's granddaughter and the beauty's niece. An air of mystery, of blurred identities hovered about all three.

The little girl was called Serafina, but I often heard the older woman speak German to her, and the child would respond in excellent German. I had no idea where her parents were. The grandmother was a neat, prim woman who favored high-buttoning blouses and long tight skirts. She wore her hair in a severe bun and suggested a head mistress at a middle class boarding school in the provinces.

Ah, but the young one! She intrigued us. She intrigued *me*. She was a shade under six feet. On those lofty Riviera beach clogs, I had to look up to her—a distinct joy. How can I describe her legs? They were interminable. Long, elegant, delicately contoured, smooth and graceful—they ran all the way from her toes to the base of her spine. On a straight-away, she could have given a giraffe a furlong handicap and nipped him at the finish. Her flesh was dark, creamy, lustrous, gently and lovingly browned by the Riviera sun. Her satiny dark auburn hair she wore in a savage horse-tail; her amber eyes hid tantalizingly behind gem-encrusted smoked glasses. She favored lavish beachwear—immense yellow raffia hats, exotic courtesan's sandals, a variety of pink, aqua and chartreuse coats, and the shortest, tightest shorts I have ever stared at.

A brief digression is in order here on the subject of the shorts worn by Italian ladies at beach resorts. Your *signorina* or *signora* wears them very short indeed, painfully tight—perhaps a size too small. The purpose is to leave exposed those two curvilinear creases of flesh that separate butt from thigh. On a warm afternoon in Portofino, a man seated at a sidewalk cafe, sipping his vermouth, gets the sense that he is surrounded by a sea of jiggling pink-brown half moons.

I never learned the charmer's name. She was not notably friendly, and spent very little time at Casa Stoppani. One day, her mother advised me primly that her daughter had a locker at the Palazzo Hotel, Rapallo's most luxurious. This news pleased me. I was glad that "Legs"—as we had named her—had an income of her own, probably from a successful modelling career.

Good old Legs! How she brightened my fly-specked mornings on the malodorous banks of the What-A-Stink River! I would pretend to be writing at my wobbly bridge table on the patio, inhaling the hot fragrance of sewage, and wishing Marie well as she set out on her morning adventure with the Citroen on the goat path. Then Legs would appear, en route to the Palazzo. Unashamedly, I would gawk. Sometimes I wished her a sly *bonjour*. She rarely responded. Shy, she was, and properly aloof. She was a girl of quality, I was certain.

82

Along about 1:00 pm, Legs would return from her beach club, usually with a gentleman friend. They varied, her callers. There were ruddy-faced Anglo-Saxons with ginger mustaches, stout Italian *borghese* with hooded eyes, furtive Frenchmen in pointed black shoes and black silk sox, Germans in *lederhosen* and thick-soled hiking boots.

"Isn't it nice," I said to Marie, as we sprawled, enervated on the patio, "that Legs has so many friends?"

"Friends? She's the unfriendliest character I've ever met. She won't give me the time of day. Not a *buongiorno*—nothing. Looks right past me."

"She's shy, poor thing," I said. "All those men who come to visit with her! Different ones every day. I guess the old lady is a great cook. They all come around lunch time, stay a couple of hours and then go."

Marie's eyes popped. "Cook! Friends! When did you wake up? Now I get the picture—those fancy beach clothes—locker at the Palazzo—that snooty manner! Who else could snub me like that except a—a—"

"No!" I cried. "Don't say it! Not my beloved Legs!"

I resented her crudity. As witness to my belief in Legs' purity, I called over Filomena, the little Rapallese girl who had succeeded Mavis as our maid. Filomena was 22, pretty, shrewd and competent. She had the confidence of a young woman who has it made—engaged to a prosperous gent who owned a bar in Sestri Levante.

"I'll ask Filomena," I said to Marie. "She knows everything that goes on here. Filomena—*La Signorina* upstairs—the one with the fancy clothes. Has she ever told you what she does? Has her Mama ever spoken to you?"

Innocently, Filomena nodded. "*Si, Signor* Gren. Her Mama says she is an actress."

I leaned back smugly. "See?" I said to Marie. "The poor girl acts sociably to the tourists and you accuse her of lewd professionalism."

Marie summoned Filomena back from hanging up the wash. "Filomena—*creda Lei questo racconto?*—do you believe this story?"

Filomena exposed two gold teeth in a sly grin. "Oh, certainly I do, *Signora*. She's an actress—with her *legs*."

They were both against me—two moralistic, jealous women. But I still had faith in Legs; I would listen to no more slander.

But Casa Stoppani was disaster-prone, and one hot August night, my wife's mean suspicions were, I am afraid, confirmed. Contrary to the popular belief in America, Italians are extremely quiet people in their homes. Vespas belch and Fiats snort in the street, but in the castle of his house or apartment, the Italian likes it still and calm. Stupefied with pasta and wine by 2:00 pm, he has little energy left for anything but sleep. By nightfall, they are as tranquil as spayed cats. One's slumber is rarely disturbed by noisy brawling, screaming argument, the general *sturm und drang* of the urban multiple dwelling. Indeed, there is very little *laughter* among the middle and upper classes in Italy. So proud are they of their high estate, that they are fearful that a laugh may involve a surrender of dignity. Only the poor laugh in Italy. It is just about all they are allowed to do. In sum, nocturnal noise usually signifies catastrophe—a burning television set, the birth of a child, a theft.

Consequently, when we were awakened by female shrieks at 2:00 am one morning, we were ready for another tragedy in Casa Stoppani. Recalling my heroism of the night of the burning TV, I leaped from my hard bed and raced to the staircase in the corridor separating our two apartments. From the first landing, Officer Lentini, Biretta in hand, called to me.

"*Guarda, Professore!*—be careful!" Lentini whispered. He then informed me his gun was unloaded. "Stay below—we are all in danger!"

"What's happening?" I called up.

"In the apartment of the young woman—a giant Negro! A cannibal! He may be armed! Who knows what he is doing to that poor girl!"

Lentini's account (I wondered why he didn't go upstairs and save her from the marauder) was interrupted by more shrieks. Suddenly an espresso pot ricocheted off the stairway walls, shattering into its component parts. It was an unwashed espresso pot, and the sticky grounds streaked Lentini's immaculate white tunic. More screams; then an assortment of spiked shoes; an antipasto of fruit and vegetables; the granddaughter's stuffed panda; a bottle of Bigi Orvieto; and finally, a tall, extremely black man, bounding down the steps like a middle distance runner, protecting his head and face from the barrage.

Lentini thoughtfully flicked on the hall light. In its 15 watt glare I beheld the fugitive—a citizen of one of the newly emerged people's republics of Africa. He wore an embroidered orange pillbox hat and a flowing purple robe. He was the color of Coco-Marsh, bespectacled and wore a pair of white Keds. As he dodged kitchenware and tomatoes, he shouted his diplomatic protests:

"*S'il vous plaît! S'il vous plaît! Non plus! Je pars!*—Please! No more! I'm going!"

Lentini levelled the Biretta at him. "Stop. Alt. *Io sono Lentini della Polizìa!*"

Knowing that the weapon was unloaded, I pushed Lentini's

hand down. "Let him go, Lentini," I said. "He is probably a prince, or a Prime Minister, and you will create an international incident. Remember what happened to your countryman at Addis Ababa!"

Lentini nodded and reluctantly lowered the Biretta. *"Vai vìa—get lost!"* he shouted at the African.

"Merci, merci!" the nocturnal visitor responded. *"Elles sont complètement folles!—*They're all nuts!"

The Negro fled into the star-spangled Riviera night. The last I saw of him, he had mounted a Vespa scooter and was blasting off down the river road, his purple robe flying behind him.

I followed Lentini upstairs. The door to Legs' apartment was open. Mother and daughter were having an old-fashioned Bronx *geshrei*. Apparently Mama had been doing the hurling—she held an egg whisk in her hand.

"Dirty girl!" the mother shouted. "Bringing blacks into this house!"

"You old hen!" Legs cried. "He's as good as anyone—and he's got better manners than those cheap *borghese* or those fat Germans!"

"He's black!" shrieked Mama.

"He's the Minister of Finance in his country!" countered Legs.

"Hah! Cannibal—that's what he is! What a sight for your poor old mother to see when she wakes up—that black giant—using my bathroom! Why must you bring home savages? Aren't there enough nice Swedes and Germans in Rapallo?"

"He's a college graduate! A professor!" Legs protested. "He was willing to pay me double what the others—"

At this point, Mama slapped her. Lentini, abashed, beckoned to me to leave. He could make his report in the morning. Meanwhile, his lower middle-class Calabrian sensitivities were offended. Indeed, mine were too—middle class Nassau County, that is. Legs had betrayed me.

And yet—how could I be too critical of her commerce? In a way, she was a kind of One-Weapon European Common Market. Her vision extended to the emerging nations, the under-developed areas that need our goodwill and our technical know-how, so that they may reach our own high estate.

Stumbling back to bed, I thought of Kurtz dying in the Heart of Darkness, of Conrad's horrid vision of Africa. It didn't help me sleep. Europe is surrealist. It is absurd—if you prefer Camus to Dali. I consoled myself with Legs' muted tolerance—as opposed to Mama's loud bigotry. My heroine had proved to me that the Western World has much to offer our dark brothers.

CHAPTER eight

Checkovich and his friends

At long last we were to taste *La Dolce Vita*—the sweet, high life. Our guide would be a man named Milo Checkovich. Once, in Portofino, Marie had said to me: "Who of all the people we know would be the most likely to turn up here?" Unhesitantly, I responded: "Checkovich." He did.

Milo Checkovich plays the role of a shabby Mephistopheles in my life, and, I suspect, in the lives of many plodding dullards like myself. His is a name automatically associated with Fire Island, St. Tropez, Deauville, Portofino, Positano and Malibu. I see him forever, prowling some sandy strand, a stubby, chubby, bearded Satan, his shrewd Serbian eyes on the prowl for innocents.

Checkovich needs some explaining. Shortly after World War II he wrote an extremely funny account of his career as a merchant seaman. His book was serialized, dramatized for television, made into an hilarious film. He never wrote anything else. Frugally husbanding his wealth, avoiding marriage, property and other entrapments, he has since created for himself an enviable role—the Professional Celebrity.

The only other Professional Celebrity I ever knew was a chimpanzee—J. Fred Muggs. Actually, the comparison is an unfair one. Muggs was exposed daily to the public; he had behind him the power of a network, battalions of publicity men and press agents. Check, on the other hand, has done it all on his own. He is the essence of our national craving for celebrities.

Marie and I first met him at Fire Island. I was flattered when he recognized me from my photo on the dust jacket of *The Last Angry Man.* He came upon me, in that odd stooped prowl, as I was changing David's diaper on a beach mat.

Two ill-tempered miniature poodles flitted around Checkovich's thick shanks. At the sight of Nancy and Teddy, the dogs made for them, chasing them off the beach. (I have since discovered this kind of thing to be characteristic of certain beach resorts—Fire Island, Westhampton, Fregene, Malibu. At all these places, nasty little poodles have chased my children away.)

There is something about miniature barbered poodles and people who own and love them that intimidates me. At once, I apologized to Check for my kids' erratic behavior. By running, they gave off an odor of adrenalin, and thereby incensed his dogs. And naturally, they had shown fear because of various insecurities for which I was responsible. As I battled David for the rubber over-pants, slipping them over his chubby legs with brute strength, my visitor agreed.

"Don't feel too bad," Checkovich said. "They ain't my poodles. I borrowed them from Lennie and Sandra."

I was properly impressed with Lennie and Sandra (who were they?) and with a man who would borrow poodles. Soon, I learned that Checkovich borrowed everything. He was a mendicant monk, living on alms, leavings, scraps, unused or unusable properties. I think all he ever owned was a flatulent MG and a pair of leopardskin bathing trunks.

"A helluva book you wrote, kiddy," he said, squatting next to me. "I liked it—even though that old doctor is a kinda shlock figure. Like you know—the sentimental old crank with the heart of gold. Too bad the reviews murdered you—maybe it was a *hack* job, but I mean, there's hack and hack."

I studied my new friend: a unique fellow, no question. His body was volley-ball round, generously muscled, as brown as Ipswich pine stain. His head was proportionately spheroid, crowned with tight golden curls, in the manner of late Greek statuary. His eyes popped slightly; they were sea green. A wispy blond beard endowed Check with the look of an early church father gone wrong. In a rather commanding way, he was ugly and handsome simultaneously.

"Checkovich is my name. Milo Checkovich," he said, in harsh New York accents. "Man, am I glad to meet a writer out here. The dump is loaded with cloak-and-suiters and dentists."

I had read *his* book and I had enjoyed it. He dusted away my praise and informed me he was collaborating on a novel that summer with a lavishly wealthy junk dealer. The scrap merchant was putting him up for the entire summer—free.

"A *quid-pro-quo*," Checkovich explained. "I give the guy a little class. He's got a real live writer on the premises. He can brag to all his deductible friends we're working on a book. Also, I'm his entrée into show biz, the literary world. I fill his house with celebrities."

This pattern, I learned, was Check's mode of existence. He was like a young male Elsa Maxwell—bringing the Great together with the Near-Great and the Would-Be-Great. How else could his scrap metal dealer ever get to rub thighs with important people like television actresses, advertising agency copywriters, off-Broadway set designers and press agents? Checkovich provided the service. He knew everyone. He was not only a name dropper, but a resort-dropper, a city-dropper and a multiple choice-dropper. When Check told you he had just had dinner with *Mel,* you were left wondering whether it was Allen, Douglas or Tormé. When he advised you he was awaiting an important phone call from Serge, you jealously tried to guess which one—Rubenstein, Semenenko or Lifar.

Certain friends of this absurd Serb contended he was unhappy. "Poor Check," they would say, "he's miserable because he stopped writing after that smash hit." Their sympathy always seemed to me misplaced. Checkovich was one of the most sublimely contented men I have ever known. He had the world licked. Brightening the world's gaudy watering spots, never spending, ever welcome, brightening summer homes and villas, he catalyzed that sprawling, glittering bauble I call the Celebrity Complex.

At once, he sensed my envy of him, my simpleton's jealousy of his freewheeling, ocean-hopping life. In that first crucial encounter on the beach at Fire Island, he acknowledged my admiration, and he tried to help me.

"Sell your Plymouth," he said. "Stop diapering this kid and looking after the others when your wife's at the beauty parlor. Get your name in Hy Gardner's column. Ever smoke pot?"

"What pot?" I asked, seeing David go under a bone-cracking wave. I started after him, but Check grabbed me.

"The kid'll make it on his own." He was right—David was washed ashore like an old Four Roses bottle.

"*Pot,* stupid," Checkovich explained. "Gauge, Muggles, Meserole. Tea. Kiddy—look what it did for Norman. He wrote about it. Can't keep out of the newspapers."

Norman who? Armour? Talmadge? Feldman? So humiliated was I that I never found out.

His challenge disturbed me. It underscored my essential failing—the power to project an image. Check had mastered it; so had J. Fred Muggs; so had Norman. Thus, when I encountered Checkovich in Portofino—inevitably—all these musings came back to me.

Marie and I had been invited to Frank Fleer's house in Portofino. Fleer is a successful magazine writer. He and his wife collaborate on terrifying articles entitled *Your Teeth Are Digging Your Grave* or *Is Your Mortgage Booby-Trapped?*

Fleer and his wife Alice, who deserve some sort of medal for guts, spent an entire summer in Portofino. Their home was a cliff-hanging castle, high, high above the tiny village with its fish-fry odors and 64-cent ice-cream cones. Their eyrie was breath-taking: a miniature palace nestling amid parasol pines— private, cool, inaccessible. It had but one drawback. No auto, no scooter, no mule could ascend the winding narrow path to the house. One went on one's feet—or not at all. A half hour was good time for the vertical climb. On reaching the summit, guests immediately developed symptoms of coronary thrombosis. Luckily, the Fleers were skin-diving that summer, and Frank was ever-ready to greet visitors with a martini in one hand and an oxygen tank and breathing mask in the other. The writer himself, a kind and considerate man, would spend the first half hour apologizing to his guests. (I felt less badly about my own lack of condition when I made the climb with Fleer one night. Frank, who is always in excellent physical shape, was gasping like a badly pummeled middleweight when we reached the house.)

That evening, when my aorta had stopped throbbing, I gave Marie a good bawling out. "Look at the Fleers!" I cried. "Are they living on the banks of the *Che Puzza* River surrounded by snails and Calabrian policemen? No! They have a castle! They live the way writers are supposed to live!"

Fleer favored me with a scowl. "I hate it here," he said.

We collapsed, feet bruised and legs scarred, our bodies quivering, too weary to complain. As we rested there, reflecting on the glories of Riviera life, a blond beard and a curly head materialized. It was Milo Checkovich, in cerise clam-diggers and lavender espadrilles, leering, sizing us up for what we were. Neither of us was surprised. Portofino-Checkovich. They went together.

Marie greeted him with restraint. She regards Check as a bad influence, a cheapjohn Satan, trying to buy my ragged soul, to lead me to dark, degraded ways. She is particularly suspicious of him ever since she learned he is from Brooklyn. Indeed, he is from a street where her father was once the cop on the beat, and she suspects that Check, long before his career as an international pet, was a street-corner loafer who tormented her Daddy. (My own suspicions are different. To me, Check has always had something in him of the poolroom galoot whom my father-in-law always whipped into line with a few thumps on the elbows.)

93

Never had Check seemed blonder, fatter, more completely in harmony with his environment. He *belonged* to Portofino.

Fleer and I are fairly good talkers—loud, opinionated, rude. But that evening, Checkovich left us at the post. What a mad time he was having that summer! Deauville, Monte Carlo, Klosters, Positano, Rhodes. And everywhere, he had been welcomed with joyous shout. And by everyone—Irwin, Kirk, Tola, Budd, Billy, Binky and Brigitte. With such as these had he supped and savored small talk. Dino wanted him to write a screenplay for Gina and Marlon. He had a deal going with Meg and Tony.

As I listened to Checkovich, a shark of envy ate my feet and started on my legs. I had flown the coop of suburban stodginess, of humdrum middleclass America, for the exotic delights of Europe—epitomized in the enchanted names of Portofino and Rapallo—and I was still a child-beating, tax-paying, anxiety-ridden worm. Checkovich was the paragon. He was all I could never be. He knew Irwin and Kirk and Tola. He was lusted after by continental beauties. Movie deals were hurled at him by Serge and Dino and several people named Hakim. Casually, he put in appearances at St. Tropez. And he wore cerise clam-diggers.

No longer could I bear his recital of his own especial *Dolce Vita*. "I want to be like you!" I cried. "Please, Mephistopheles! Take me along! I slept last night with three of my son's pet snails! My other son cries for peanut butter sandwiches—and we've bought all the peanut butter in Rapallo—imported from England at exorbitant prices! My daughter Nancy hollers for Janet! Do something for me, Satan—make me a part of your mad, mad world!"

Strangely, Marie agreed. "Go ahead, Check—take over. That'll teach the boob."

The corrupter was delighted. At once, he announced to Fleer and myself that he would arrange a party in our honor. And what a party! Fodor could supply the adjectives—*gay, mad, snobbish, chi-chi, alluring.* The festa would be in honor of the American literary colony—Fleer, Green and himself. He would honor a local Contessa who adored him, by letting her be the hostess. A wild night of drinking, dining, wenching and unsupervised free-play was promised.

Ingratitude is a trait I decry in others, and I try to suppress it in myself. And Checkovich's Contessa treated us nobly—far better than we deserved. So the account I now present of my introduction to *La Dolce Vita,* must come under the heading of ungrateful boorishness by a rude American to a friendly allied nation. Let me say the worst things first. The mad, gay, wild night was a monument of dullness, propriety, boredom and good manners. Fellini—where are you? *La Dolce Vita,* I suspect, is largely invention—a sweet, degraded, corrupt life that looms large in its creator's imagination, a kind of onanistic orgy. Or was it me? Were all these Italian and Western European *hautmonde* types forced into a mould of blandness and innocence by my square (*quadrato*) presence? We shall never know.

Surely the setting was conducive to a frothy night of revels. The Contessa's villa was tucked away in a secret wave-washed cove, hidden behind high yellow walls, girt round with a lavish garden of delights—ivy, fern, palms, exquisite little mosaic benches, unexpected tile patios, balconies, summer houses, and pools where goldfish undulated. Lanterns aflame with exotic colored light festooned the grape arbors. Indentured Genovese servants moved silently among us serving cold seafood antipasto. Perhaps it was the Coca-Cola I requested that put the damper on everything; perhaps it was because Check wandered off with an actress and her poodles; but all I recall of the festa was an atmosphere as exhilarating as Mme. Tussaud's.

The hostess, I am forced to admit, was charming. She was a beauty in her 50's—a former model, comedienne, collector of husbands. She was working on her fifth, a Milanese banker, who was absent. I remarked that it was inconceivable that a sane man could leave a charmer like herself alone in Portofino; she shrugged and told me: "But that is what summers are for. For husband and wife to get away from one another. And I am hardly alone." With a sweep of her edible white arm, she took in the assemblage of important people.

I must now describe some of them—Checkovich's circle.

There was an Englishman, titled and somewhat tilted to sea-ward, who was intrigued with Albania. He was an arrow-thin, soaring man, with an askew blond head and a disturbing habit of mutilating vowels and slicing consonants. He was largely un-intelligible; in his case the U-accent had reached point of no re-turn. I could not feel inferior to him, because I understood very little of what he said. Unlike the sober-sided Italians, he got drunk quite early in the evening and proceeded to harangue me about the coming freedom of Albania. I agreed that Albania should be free; I deplored the Communist tyranny in Eastern Europe.

"Ay'm organizing an Army of Exiles to march into Albania," his lordship piped. "Would you be int'rested?"

I explained I was not an Albanian.

"Oh. That would make a difference, wouldn't it?"

Then he told me of his plot to restore King Zog to the throne. (The monarch is since deceased, and so missed his last chance).

Zog would be smuggled into the country disguised as a goose girl. At the National Agricultural Fair at Tirana, the blond wig would be ripped off, and the peasants would acclaim him again.

Paraphrasing Jack Dempsey, I told his lordship that perhaps the good king lost his throne because "he zigged when he should have zogged."

There was a heavy silence. Then he exploded with Hogarthian laughter: "Jolly Good!" he cackled. "Jolly Good Show! Zigged when he should have zogged!"

The trouble with this kind of Englishman—Italy is filled with them—is that they dilute my natural Anglophilia. Listening to Albania's champion, talking in deadly serious vein about the coming invasion of Albania by exiles disguised as goose girls, I begin to wonder how my favorite foreign country turned out Dr. Johnson, Churchill and Jem Mace. Moreover, I am disturbed about the future of the countries under Red oppression. Isn't there anyone besides these oddballs who are available to help in the liberation? I suppose there is; somehow I never seem to meet them.

On the distaff side, the Contessa's party featured a variety of extremely wealthy Torinese and Milanese ladies—sporty types in turquoise Capri pants and chartreuse blouses. Marie and I have given these people the generic name of *simperers*. They were very rich ladies, indeed, of different ages, shapes and sizes, distinguished by a varnished exterior, half-shut eyes, arched plucked brows, and an inability to laugh, smile, react, or enjoy anything beyond a contemplation of their own splendid persons. They were dummies: the women of Italy's leaders. (Reprimanding voice: Green, aren't you being too harsh? They can't be that unemotional. Didn't you catch two of these ladies holding hands under a trellis? Answer: yes, but they were probably just cold).

I remember particularly one vivacious Austrian woman in her thirties, without escort, I gathered, a beauty in dirndl and blond braids (not a goose girl) who tossed off her sandals and challenged several men to a forty yard dash across the barbered lawn. Since no one accepted her challenge, she began making goo-goo eyes at one of the Contessa's white-coated serfs. Whether this developed into a new Tyrolean entente, I never found out.

By far my favorite guest at Checkovich's High Life party, was an Arab. He was a rich Arab, an assumption one can make for any Arab who turns up in Italy, especially Portofino. His name was Habib, and he had a rather close connection with the oil revenues flooding into the Middle East. As we sat on the lantern-lit lawn, munching squid and shrimp, seeking for subjects of discussion other than Simonetta and Lollobrigida (Moravia got a few calls, but I doubt that any there had read him) I found myself attracted to Habib Pasha, and sat down beside him.

He was a small, thick fellow, with lavish black burnsides and hooded eyes. In his shiny black silk suit and white tie, he would have been much at home at a ringside table at the Copacabana. I introduced myself. Habib studied me warily. That evening, I suspected, after bathing and shaving, he had anointed his round, well-nourished face with sandalwood oil. No diets of dried dates cooked over camel dung for him, thank you.

"You are a Jew?" he asked suddenly. He asked it not with malice, or suspicion, but as if wanting to set the record straight.

"I am."

He sighed. "It is inevitable. Always, I end up with members of the Hebrew tribe for conversational partners."

"Look here," I said testily, "we're on neutral ground. Why

get nasty about it? You start with the insults, I have a few myself. What about the way four Haganah soldiers took the Arab camp at Beit Sfafa—a whole division surrendered! And there was that time at Tulkarm when—"

"Plizz." He held up a be-ringed, hairy hand. "That is what I mean. I did not insult you. I merely mentioned I always have to talk to Jews. I don't mind. I just am tired of discussing politics. War, Zionism—I'm sick of them. We can never agree, so why argue? Now what do you wish to discuss? Women? Italy? Movies?"

His frankness pleased me, and I told him so. Habib modestly accepted my praise. "I come to Italy for pleasure, not debates," he said. "Is that not a reasonable attitude?"

"It is! It is!" I said enthusiastically. He seemed a thoroughly decent chap—prosperous, friendly in a saturnine way. And I rather enjoyed his accent—it brought back misty memories of my boyhood in Brooklyn—memories of kosher delicatessens and pushcart markets, of Turkish baths and halvah. Semitic brotherhood was no myth; it was true.

Unfortunately, our attempts at conversation lagged. I tried first to draw him out—what he did for a living, where he lived, what brought him to Portofino—but he was evasive and diffident. Like many Middle Eastern pashas and Latin American *hidalgos* floating around Italy, he was just plain rich, no explanations offered. So I tried a new approach, one which I imagined to be a brilliant one.

"Yes, you're right, Habib Pasha," I said, as *La Dolce Vita* buzzed about me—Checkovich, barefoot, in zebra shirt and gold pants, doing a snakey rhumba with an octogenarian Torinese *Principessa*—"we should be friends and not irritate one another."

99

Silent, he nodded, sipping his *Punt E Mes,* a delectable bitter vermouth, highly prized by connoisseurs. It tastes like Pertussin.

"For example," I went on, "our peoples have lived in harmony for many centuries." I racked my brain for an example, catching the nasal whine of the skinny Englishman as he shilled for King Zog to an audience of wax-work women. "Take the middle ages," I said. "It is well known that Hebrew communities prospered and were given favored status under Arab rulers. They supplied doctors and philosophers for the courts of Islam, no?"

Habib was not terribly impressed with my overture to brotherhood. He waved his hand, but I would not quit. What other nice things could I say about the Arabs? "Algebra!" I suddenly shouted—drawing the puzzled stares of a Sicilian landed baron who favored a white lily in his lapel.

"Algebra?" asked Habib.

"Sure! Everyone knows *you* invented Algebra. And Arithmetic! And numbers! Where would we all be without Arabic numerals? Two, four, six, eight—who do we appreciate? The Arabs, the Arabs! Sis-boom-bah!"

Now he smiled. "You are amusing," he said.

"Oh, but that isn't all," I said, warming up. "Think of all the Arab cultural contributions to the world! Look at Spain— their architecture, their art—all Arabic! Toledo—Granada— Seville—why, they'd never have amounted to a bowl of *paella* without the Arabs!"

I suddenly realized I was running out of testimonials. Worse, he was bored with my high praise. Unfortunately, I am cursed with a good memory for names, and a few popped into my mind.

"And let's not forget Averroes! And Avicenna! Two great Arabs!" Now I was shouting. The Contessa, our generous host, glided towards us, a vision in yards of pale green Simonetta gown and seven strands of pearls.

"*Che cosa*—what's up?" she asked, in a delectable fluty voice. "Is *Signor* Gren fighting with you Habib, *carissima?*"

"No, no," the rich Arab said. "He is amusing."

"Yes sir!" I yelled, as she departed, "we owe the Arabs plenty! Averroes and Avicenna were two darn good doctors! Why, you could draw a straight line of medical progress all the way from them right down to Dr. Morris Fishbein!"

Habib drained his vermouth. Under the multi-colored lanterns he seemed as wise, as discreet as Harun Al-Rashid. He had true presence, and I wondered if he had ever commanded a rifle platoon in the Gaza Strip, or performed terrorist missions for the old fox, Fawzi Al-Kawukji.

"What you say is very true, my dear Semite brother," Habib Pasha said. "Very true. Your praise of my people is acknowledged. We have indeed contributed much to an ungrateful world. But shall I inform you of one magnificent Arab achievement of which you know nothing? Nothing at all? An achievement which makes everything you have mentioned shrink to the size of a sand fly?"

"Tell me, oh learned one!" I cried. "I must know! After all, a people who gave us algebra and astronomy—"

The palm of his pudgy hand halted me. He had had quite enough of my testimonials. "My friend, some day you will come to Alexandria with me," he said enigmatically, and halted.

Yes, yes! I will go to Alexandria with you Habib! I will be the Nassau County Lawrence Durrell! I will out-Checkovich Checkovich!

"And when we go to Alexandria, my friend," Habib continued, "I will escort you to an establishment, a palace of pleasure. And there you will see performed *every kind of sexual perversion known to man!* What do you say to that?"

"Ah—ah—it's a challenge," I stammered.

"And whom do you think invented these variations of love? Who perfected these infinite attitudes and specialties? We did! The Arabs! That is our greatest contribution to culture! Think of something new. Don't bother—we Arabs have already thought of it. And we have generously given it to the world."

"You—you wouldn't kid me, would you Habib?" For a moment I thought of challenging him with *Sanctuary*.

"We are past joking. You spoke of Arab contributions to the world. So, I have told you of the greatest. Arithmetic. Algebra. Pah! Nothing. And who is to say what is perverse and what is not perverse?"

I was delighted to discover that he was a relativist, in addition to being rich and friendly. By now I was embarrassed by my meagre, sterile praise of the Arabs.

"I—I grant you that, Habib," I said. "But there *is* vice and virtue to consider. As Dr. Johnson once said, if a man says there is no difference between them, let us count the spoons when he leaves our house."

"Typical narrow puritanical American outlook."

"Dr. Johnson was English."

"Worse yet. Need I tell you how many Englishmen I have taken to that palace in Alexandria?" He got up, weary of our strained relationship. "The next time people ask you what we Arabs have given to mankind, remember what I have just told you. It makes for better conversation than arithmetic."

So saying, Habib Pasha waddled off.

Alone, I reflected on his boasts. How I admired him! What candor—what innocence! The glorification of one's ethnic origins is always a problem fraught with pitfalls. What German would dare cite Hitler or Himmler as representative of his nation, in preference to a Goethe or a Beethoven? Surely the vast majority of Frenchmen would call on a Pasteur or a Cézanne, before Gobineau or Robespierre, as evidence of national glory. Ah—but how many—French, Germans, Americans—secretly admire the bad guys? How many nurture dark yearnings for a Dillinger—as opposed to a Jefferson?

But Habib Pasha was no hypocrite. To him, the fleshpots of wicked Alexandria, those ancient Arab experimenters and innovators, were dearer to his Levantine heart than all the mathematics texts and prescriptions of the old Islamic philosophers.

His revelations were the high-water mark of the evening. I gazed about at the *Dolce Vitalities* around me. The view was depressing in the extreme. There was a hum of low, bored voices, an occasional insincere laugh. No one was drunk. There was less kissing, smooching and necking than goes on at a chaperoned high school graduation party in Lake Ronkonkoma, New York.

I toured the lawn looking for trouble.

Marie and Alice Fleer were having a fierce argument about proportional representation.

Fleer, my magazine writer, was explaining to three sleepy ladies of quality about his new series for a woman's magazine. It would be called, he confided: *Change of Life—Challenge and Chastisement.* He was having trouble getting it into Italian.

And so our evening dribbled on. At one point I seem to remember discussing cholesterol with a man who claimed to be the only medical dietician in Padua. I confess he intrigued me— as do all highly specialized, individualized persons. At International News Service we once had an Argentinian who claimed to be the only man ever to get a medical discharge from the French Foreign Legion. He enlisted for five years to forget—and it took him only two years.

Checkovich had fallen asleep on the Contessa's private dock. The Austrian woman in the dirndl and his lordship—still explaining his Free Albania plan—were trying to revive him by forcing Strega between his lips. Hours later, I recall, everyone drove off to a beach-front night club in Santa Margherita where we listened to fractured rock-and-roll, and Habib Pasha sprung for champagne for everyone. The oil business must have been good that summer.

Around me, in Capri pants, in knee-length sweaters, in yellows and purples and greens, the high-spirited, racy international set of the Italian Riviera, bubbled and babbled and stared—Fodor's 400. Theirs was the timeless boredom and emptiness of privilege. And as I sat there, nursing a Coca-Cola, I thought of Trotsky. Only a few hundred yards from where I sat, that caustic pamphleteer had—only 37 years ago—signed the Treaty of Rapallo with the Germans. How Trotsky would have smiled and approved of all of us! His bearded, bespectacled ghost would have nodded, and perhaps revived his old comment on the Czar's daily round of activities—before the earth heaved:

All on the very border-line of physiology.

But this, I would hope, is essentially a light-hearted book, with no room for a ghostly Bolshevik in it. Yet the spook of Trotsky haunted me that night when I encountered Europe's elite, and it haunts me still.

Pover' Italia; nothing will be gained by another recounting of what ails that much-loved country . . . a lack of social justice, a dearth of social conscience, a resistance to rationalism, an absence of plain good sense and fair play. But whatever problems she has are problems that are magnified a thousandfold in those vast, dark areas of the world where people do not eat enough. And why is it I keep asking myself, we usually end up with people like the Contessàs friends—when the *other* side is taught and led by the tough, brutal, shrewd pupils of Trotsky? Does it not appear we have been over-matched—unless we can find other horses to back?

I do not relish the notion of my grandchildren having to learn to be laundrymen in a regimented, humorless, arid world run by the *others*—simply because we and our associates are too full of good times to have resisted.

CHAPTER nine

sophisticati

Among the Myths about Italy that must be exposed, is the one that insists "you can live cheaply there."

Possibly one can live cheaply in Western Sicily, in a mountain village surrounded by cacti, Mafia and impoverished, brutalized peasants. But in any section of Italy where the largesse of the tourist has influenced the citizenry, living tends to be expensive —especially for the foreigner. I do not mean only the expenses of tourism—but the daily costs of food, housekeeping, and so forth.

In simplest terms, the high cost of living reflects the Italian mercantile leadership's concept of a sound economy—a small volume of business, an excess of retail outlets, exorbitant mark-ups. It is a system that would terrify any rational American free enterprise capitalist. And it applies to everything from pasta to automobiles.

On one residential street, for example, there will be seven food stores—duplicating one another, overlapping, each claiming a widow's mite of the market. One store will sell baked goods, eggs, and soap; another will sell cold cuts, cheese, canned goods and eggs; a third, pasta, eggs, bread and cookies; a fourth, milk, ice-cream, cookies, eggs and candy. There are no hard and fast lines of demarcation, and even the unbeatable Mavis could not satisfactorily differentiate for me *Rosticerrìas, Salumerìas, Salsamenterìas, Drogherìas, Panifìcios, Pasticerrìas, Pizzicherìas,* and so on. Each little food store will have a limited stock, an even more limited clientèle, and will mark up the price of its wares so high, as to inhibit purchasing power, mass buying, inducements to the customers. Italian automobiles are sold the way food is—an enormous margin of profit, a limited volume.

A curious turnabout must be noted here. While retail trade in Italy is a shambles—a confusion of overlapping stores, dupli-cation, cut-throat competition which does nothing to benefit the consumer—the big producers of goods are few, powerful, well-organized and often monopolistic.

In any event, we were soon disabused about living cheaply in Italy. Rapallo, a resort, was one of the most expensive places in the country. Rome was an improvement, but one could never escape the feeling that it was a losing battle. To begin with, cooks traditionally order the food. It is considered bad form for the lady of the house to shop for food, order it on the phone, or even enter the kitchen—except to make sure the refrigerator is locked. (Italian *borghese* lock the refrigerator to discourage theft.

It is opened only to take out the day's needs, then shut tighter than the vault at Chase Manhattan).

The cook immediately negotiates an *entente cordiale* with the local food merchants—the baker, grocer, fruiterer, milkman—in which the householder is obligated to pay reparations to all signatories. The householder is never informed of this pact, he is merely obliged to accept it. Thus, the cook will order twice as much food as necessary, and the merchant will charge twice as much as the local Italians pay. The indemnities levelled on the employer are then shared on a steal-as-you-go basis. (I hasten to add that this kind of economic planning was observed only in Rome. In Rapallo, Mavis would not allow it—to the anger of Assunta—and little Filomena was also scrupulously honest).

Once in Rome, Marie tried to beat the system by shopping at the supermarket. She soon quit. Just about everything she bought there was thrown out, hidden or taken home as a war prize by the cook.

Meats were exorbitant and inedible. A row of plucked Italian chickens hanging by their necks, scrawny and white-ruffed, invariably reminded me of Plato's mean characterization of man—that unfeathered fowl. There was lots of veal—tough and stringy; almost no beef worthy of the name; and occasionally some good spring lamb. We became great partisans of pasta, in its manifold shapes, served with a variety of sauces. Indeed, we soon learned that pasta fabricated from Italian wheat has a subtler, richer taste than the American variety. I suspect it has something to do with the sun and the soil.

(My wife, claiming that her Italian ancestry gives her an added insight into these matters, has long contended that the different *shapes* of macaroni give them different tastes. "Impossible," I always say. "The shapes may be different, but the flour is the same." "They taste different," she says, infuriating me. "The shape does it—linguini tastes different than capellini, which is different in taste from ziti or mezzani or maruzze—" Then I get apoplectic. "Look!" I scream. "The pasta is all the same! They have this great big tub of flour and water—all from the same wheat. Then they force it through different holes to make the shapes—but it is the same damn flour! Shape does not control taste!" Marie nods her head at my stupidity. "They taste different.")

A kind, nay a laudatory, word must be added about most Italian fruits and vegetables. Naturally, they come only fresh. No one opens cans or frozen boxes, and all to the good. Figs, peaches, melons, plums, cherries—they have an aroma and a texture that defies description. They have been fed no vitamins, but they burst with sunlight. One tiny fragolino—a wild strawberry the size of one's pinky nail—has more winey bouquet than the entire display of fat, flannelly strawberries in an American supermarket.

Before I begin to sound like a professional Europe-lover, let me return to my thesis. True, the fruits and vegetables were heavenly. But our food bills, especially in Rapallo, were murderous—often double what we paid in Westbury, Long Island. What helped jack up the weekly outlay was our children's refusal to abandon American eating habits. The first day *La Dottoressa* called on us (to administer a few expert shots to the boys, a chore she performed with greater skill and less pain than any pediatrician I have ever known) she sharply informed Nancy, Teddy and David:

"No more peanut butter and jelly sandwiches for you! From now on you eat pasta every day!"

La Dottoressa only succeeded in enforcing their fierce loyalty to peanut butter. True, they ate pasta—but they demanded peanut butter also. (Will someone please do a survey of the fascination this stuff has for kids? Like a relationship with toilet training?) In any event, we were blackmailed by the three kids into purchasing things like peanut butter, ketchup, Kellogg's Variety Packs, and so on. And in Italy, anything packaged— domestic or imported—is about as costly as cut diamonds. The prices generally run three times as high as the American price.

Thus, when the notorious food scandal broke, I was enraged. The Italians have a marvelous word to describe adulterated food —*sophisticati*. In the context of food, it means deceptive, fraudulent, of uncertain content. And the Italian press was filled with frightening news about *sophisticati* in foods. Two other companionate words were also employed—*frodatori* and *adulterati*— fraudulent and adulterated, but I was a confirmed *sophisticati* man from the start.

News of the nationwide scandal first appeared in the left-wing press. Promptly, the stories were picked up by the neo-fascists. This is a common procedure in Italy. On all issues relating to the public weal, the Communists and Socialists usually begin the agitation. Not to be outdone in their concern for the little man, the new Fascists get on board. Both extremes then join in virulent attacks on the great, bland Church-directed Christian Democratic party which occupies a large, but shaky middle ground, and runs the government. The Demochristians sit back with true Latin calm, listen to the screaming assaults on their integrity, and wait for the scandal to blow over. Invariably, it does.

As more and more accounts of the horrid state of affairs in food production began to enliven the newspapers, I became worried. And it seemed to me that the Italians themselves would begin to worry. Italians love their food. Even poor Italians get incredible satisfaction out of the modest diet that sustains them —pasta, bread, a bit of cheese, a piece of fragrant fruit, a glass of red wine. And above all, no matter how poor they may be, they have their *olio*—their olive oil—light, digestible, lubricatory, possessed of a mystic value beyond its mere nutritive worth.

And it was with intense horror that I realized that this very oil, this beloved *olio,* was at the heart of the *sophisticati* scandal. For, according to the press, a good deal of the olive oil consumed in Italy, was heavily enriched with *the rendered fat of mules, horses and donkeys.* One satirical weekly began printing mock advertisements for new brands of olive oil—named for famous race horses. But the adulteration scandal did not stop with the oil. Wine was being distilled from beans and figs. Rice was mixed with husks and gravel.

Depressed, I sought out a young Italian journalist I knew in Rapallo, whom I shall call Carlo. Carlo free-lanced for magazines, and had written a novel. He was a mild socialist, about as leftwing as Senator Clifford Case, but was nevertheless regarded by the local elite as a malign influence. Checkovich's Contessa, for example, had shuddered when I mentioned that the bright young Italian writer, Carlo M——, was a friend of mine. "*Sinistra*—left!" she had sneered. "A dangerous man!"

Like all intellectuals and intelligent members of the anti-Communist Left in Italy, poor Carlo felt isolated, unwanted. The extremes hold the power—either Communist or Clerical Right—and there are very few places where the likes of my journalist friend were able to earn a living, or get an audience.

Consequently, Carlo was delighted to meet me every few days at the Nettuno bar, where we would chat, sip espresso, and watch the parade of fleshy half-moons. Carlo was young, married and artistic, and he was able to supply a splendid running commentary. We both admired the high heels affected by the wearers of short shorts, the manner in which these stilts added wobble to the upper reaches of the thighs. In back of us, a Genovese hot five played rock-and-roll.

> How do Ay know?
> Da Bible tells me so!

I took this selection to be further evidence of the growth of religious tolerance in Catholic Italy. Creeping Fundamentalism was now acceptable in their popular music—with no protest from *Osservatore Romano*.

"Now about these terrible stories about adulterated foods," I said to Carlo. "Are they true?"

"Of course they're true. But it's nothing new. It's been going on for years. Most food in Italy is produced by giant combines—growers' cooperatives called *Federconsorzi*. The individual growers, I must point out, are for the most part multi-millionaire landholders—not little guys. And these *Federconsorzi* are not only heavily subsidized by the government, but pay very little taxes."

"Socialism!" I shouted.

"No, no—more like Fascism. A kind of bastard hangover."

"But about the frauds in food—the olive oil made from old mules—"

"*Paziènza*, Gren. I'm coming to that. As you see, these big shots are very powerful, very close to the government. In the Ministry of Agriculture there is a bureau for the repression of fraud in foods. There are thirteen geographical departments, each with a director."

"It sounds like a good set-up" I said.

"Ah, yes. It is too good. Six of these thirteen directors, whose job it is to detect and suppress the adulteration of food, are paid, not by the government of Italy—but by the rich growers—the *Federconsorzi!*"

"But how can the Italian people permit this!" I protested. "They love their food more than anything!"

Carlo smiled at my naivete. *"Caro* Gren, as long as nobody dies, there will be no complaints. Even then, I suspect there will be no real agitation to enforce the laws. Haven't you learned that my countrymen will put up with anything?"

"But is it true that melted down mules and horses are really going into our olive oil? The stuff I feed my children?"

Carlo laughed. "Probably—in some of it. Oh, it can't hurt them. Animal fats are perfectly all right. Last month, a reporter found out that the importation of horses, mules and donkeys into Italy for slaughter, rose almost 200 per cent in the last two years. Where is all that stuff going?"

I suffocated a nervous belch. At lunch, just a few hours earlier, Filomena had served us a delicious *fritto misto* of seafood, encrusted in flour, lovingly fried in olive oil. And there had been a pungent mixed green salad—in the same oil.

My journalist friend admired a pair of well-rounded *glutei,* nesting beneath a pair of extra-tight lavender shorts. "Ai," Carlo groaned, *"Che gioia*—what a joy." He noticed that I had not joined him in his sidewalk ecstasy. "Oh, cheer up, Gren. Look at me. I'm a Socialist, a reformer. I believe in helping the people. But I know that nothing can be done about *sophisticati,* so I accept it."

"By George, I don't accept it!" I shouted. "I don't want my kids guzzling horse-fat!"

"Oh, that whole problem may be over-stated in the press. The real adulteration of olive oil is subtler and more widespread. It involves the use of the residue from the first pressing."

"Oh? How does that work?"

"Some chemist—a few years ago in Turin—discovered you could re-press the olive pulp and eliminate the acid. This second pressing gave them an extra ten per cent of oil, but it was hardly the pure stuff. Now everybody does it."

I was getting queasier by the minute. "And the wine made from figs and beans? The rice full of gravel?"

"It is well known one can distill alcohol from any kind of sugar or starch. Why not figs or beans? A little coloring—and it's as good as most Italian wine. As for the rice, I don't know. I'm not a rice eater. That's for the Milanese. Why are you so upset? If it doesn't bother my countrymen, why should it bother you?"

Hurrying back to the Casa Stoppani, I vowed that I would wage a one-man war against the evil practitioners of *sophisticati*. If the Italians didn't care enough to protest, I would.

On the *Lungomare*, I got a glimpse of Teddy and David, looking fat and sluggish, riding in a donkey cart. It was their tenth ride of the day. Each clutched a fistful of educational gum cards. (Afghanistan: Religion—Baptist) and they licked drippy ice cream cones. I drowned in guilt for them. Selfishly, I had deracinated them from Westbury, Long Island—so that they might eat mule fat. Their innocence, their martydom demanded action on my part.

At the apartment, I interrogated Marie sharply about our foodstuffs. First, I ordered an end to the no-name red wine we were buying at 16 cents a liter. From now on, we would splurge on name brands—48 cents a bottle.

"My big worry is the oil," I said. "I don't like the idea of our

114

insalata mista being gently laved in Man O'War. Where does Filomena buy our oil?"

"From the general store—the *tabacchi*—on the corner, I imagine." She showed me a wide-necked bottle. It was one of the major national brands, a widely advertised variety. I wasn't sure whether I was consoled or not—Carlo had warned that even the big companies didn't hesitate to cut the product.

That afternoon when Filomena herded the kids back from the beach, I asked her where she was getting the oil.

"From *Signor* Lentini—the cop," she said.

"Lentini? That Calabrese? Why?" Immediately, I was furious. Lentini was an impossible busy-body—an interferer and clumsy finagler. Of all the people in the world to be involved in peddling phony oil, he was the most likely. We had dubbed him *Il Rompere-Coglioni*—He Who Fractures the Reproductive Organs.

"He has a colleague who grows his own olives and presses his own oil," Filomena said nervously. "He swears it is absolutely pure—*olio proprio*."

Coolly, I turned to my wife. "Did you authorize this?" I asked. "Are you letting her purchase oil from that Calabrian flatfoot? When this country is awash with rendered donkeys—and he probably is fencing for the donkey syndicate?"

"How do you know it's adultered?" Marie said. "It tastes delicious. It cooks marvelously. It has a nice pale green tint, the way good oil should. And I've tasted a lot more olive oil than you have—I know it's good. Would I argue with you about chicken fat?"

Ignoring her crudeness, I turned to Filomena, who seemed ready to cry. I had long suspected certain innocent trafficking between her and Lentini. She was quite pretty, and the gumshoe had been hanging around too much. His idea of a big joke was

115

to point his Biretta at her and make suggestive references to it, which she appreciated. Of course, nothing would ever come of it. In Italy, there is much lewd flirtation—and virtually no pre-marital carrying-on.

Still, I was suspicious. In my mind's eye, I had a vision of Lentini's colleague's oil factory—a monstrous rusted hopper into which were indiscriminately poured donkeys, mules, horses, ponies, zebras and wild asses, together with the pulpy residue of old pressings, and now and then an occasional fresh olive, just to satisfy the food inspector.

"What do you pay for this oil?" I asked Filomena.

"Less than in the store," she answered craftily.

"That proves it," I said to Marie. "Lentini is obviously the front man for a gigantic ring of oil adulterators, drowning Italy in rendered mule fat. And we, dumb *Americani* that we are, we encourage this miscreant by buying his equinic oil and setting a bad example for the rest of the country. Filomena—I forbid you to buy his oil. *Capito?*"

But Marie is too kind. She cannot bear offending people, even the likes of Angelo Lentini. After all, didn't he help me rescue the Citroen from the *Che Puzza* River? Didn't he have a wife and two kids to support? And besides—when did I ever complain about the oil? Our fried foods and salads were delicious. And Filomena swore it was pure.

But I would not be swayed. More than Lentini's sneaky oper-ations was at stake. All of Italy must be taught a lesson. I wanted to make an impression on all of them—not only Checkovich's parasitical friends, producing bad goods for too much money, but the vast inchoate, mute swarm, who got taken in regularly, accepted the swindle, and never protested.

"Filomena," I said firmly, "I am not angry with you. But the next time Lentini shows up with his oil, I wish to confront him."

116

Marie shook her head. "You're getting into deep water, boy. Stay out of these intra-Italian affairs. I know."

Filomena obeyed me. One morning, as I was typing in the bedroom, inhaling the fragrance of sewage and crushed snails, she rushed in. Lentini had arrived with a new shipment of olive oil.

Manfully, I strode out to the patio. There he was, in snappy white jacket and hat, gray drill pants, and insincere grin. His Calabrese face beamed with mercenary joy. He snapped off a jazzy salute.

"*Buongiorno, Professore!*" Lentini shouted. "I have brought you some more of my colleague's delicious pure olive oil! It is most healthful for the babies!"

No Italian ever eats or drinks anything without assuring himself of its health-giving qualities, particularly for children. A bottle of *aqua minerale* will list a full chemical analysis of the soda water, down to the last grain of potassium chloride, with a guarantee that regular drinking of the bubbly stuff will cure ailments of the liver, spleen, pancreas, musculature and cardiovascular system. The testimonial is always signed by a *Professore Dottore*, usually from Milan or Bologna. These labels were among my favorite lunchtime reading matter; I often wanted to write to the *Professore Dottore* for a photostat of his diploma.

"Lentini," I began cautiously, "who is this colleague who makes this oil? And how does he make it?"

"He is an honest, honorable man—my wife's cousin. I swear by the Virgin of Mont' Allegre, that it is beautiful oil. He lives on a farm fifty kilometers from Rapallo, and I go there myself to bring the oil for you. The poor man needs the money. He has three hungry children, one of whom requires an operation on his left ear because of a curse placed on it by a certain witch—"

Filomena giggled. She was a hard-headed Rapallese—cynical,

practical, reasonably well-educated. Lentini's deep belief in witches and curses—he was a southerner—amused her.

"I myself carry this great burden on to the bus, just so you, my friend the *Professore,* may have pure, sweet olive oil." He pointed to a large square bundle, wrapped in soiled burlap.

"Now listen to me, Lentini," I said. "I have nothing against you or your wife's cousin. I am sorry for the child who has the cursed ear. But as you know, there is a lot of *adulterati* in food in Italy today. I read the newspapers. One never knows what one is buying. How do I know how this oil is made? Who made it? What he puts in it? How can you guarantee to me that your wife's cousin does not dilute it with the fatty tissues of horses?"

"No!" he shouted, falling back, clutching his heart. "No! Never! I am a man of honor! So is my wife's cousin! It is pure oil! Ask Filomena! Ask your *Signora,* who has told me herself she is of Italian ancestry, and is therefore a better judge of these things than yourself!"

"But you cannot prove it to my satisfaction. I am sorry, Lentini. Take your oil."

"I will charge you less!" he cried.

"No. I am not a cruel man, but I cannot jeopardize the health of my children with donkey fat. Go."

"No, no, I beg you! I carried this oil on my back, all the way from the mountains!" He turned to Filomena. She, little baggage, was still giggling—enjoying his misery. Revenge, no doubt, for his dirty jokes with the Biretta. "Filomena—tell the *Professore!* It is pure oil, is it not? It cooks well, does it not?"

"It's all right," she said. "I've tasted better."

"See? Filomena supports me fully! She is on my side! Please, *Signor* Gren, for a price so reasonable—"

I shook my head. By teaching Lentini and his colleague a

lesson, I would perform a service for Italy. The word would get around. Soon even the huge *Federconsorzi*—the big monopolistic food producers would get the message and clean house.

As I turned my back, Lentini fell to his knees and grabbed my hand. "You cannot be so cruel! I am a poor policeman with children to feed! Ah, I know why you are punishing me like this! It has nothing to do with the oil, nothing!"

I turned. "Why am I punishing you, then?"

"Because—because—you think I am a Communist!" He glowered at Filomena. "A certain person who wishes me harm has told you I am a Communist! A lie! A lie! I am not! I am a Christian Democrat! I hate Communists!"

Haughtily, I replied: "This is not a political matter."

"Oh, I know how all you Americans feel about Communists," Lentini wailed. "You dislike them—and with good reason. I hate them also. They, who send rockets up into the air! Monsters!"

Still on his knees, he pulled a wallet from his tunic and began to throw dog-eared cards at me. "See! My membership card in the Christian Democratic Party! Hurrah for deGasperi!"

"He is dead."

"Then hurrah for whoever is the chief of the government, provided he is not a Communist! Oh, how I admire your *bella* lady—the Ambassador Mrs. Luce!"

"She is no longer ambassador."

"Then whoever is, I am for her!"

"It is a man, Mr. Zellerbach."

"I admire Mr. Zellerbach. And President Roosevelt! Eisenhower! Van Heflin! All Americans! Please, please—reconsider and buy my oil! It is pure and contains no *adulterati!*"

When he began to kiss my hand, I knew I was licked. Besides,

I could see Marie parking the car below and unloading our three grumblers. She would naturally side with Lentini.

"Very well, Lentini," I said. "But I do this only because I am a kind American. But I warn you. The first sign of illness in my family—and you are finished. If my children begin to kick like mules or bray like donkeys, I will report you to the Chief of Police for selling *sophisticati* to tourists."

At once, he stopped slobbering, retrieved his various cards from the patio, and ran off—leaving the burlap-wrapped bundle. Filomena lugged it into the kitchen. Marie climbed wearily up the steps.

"Well?" she asked. "Did you cut him off?"

How could I explain that the wily cop had put me in the position of opposing our government's foreign policy, denying an ear operation to a poor farmer's child, and acting like a fiend?

We resumed using Lentini's olive oil. The food still tasted fine. No one got ill or developed equine tendencies. My own face, at best, resembles Native Dancer in repose, and the change would never be noticed. After a few days, I admitted reluctantly to Marie that perhaps our Calabrese lawman had not lied. Maybe his wife's cousin's oil was pure, at that.

Wandering through the kitchen one day, I saw Filomena decanting oil from a large, squarish can to the store bought oil bottles. A mate to the large can rested on the floor. Both containers were quite dirty, and were painted with a vertical tricolor —wide bands of blue, white and red. In the white band there appeared a familiar name:

ESSO

My voice quavered. "Filomena, is that Lentini's oil?"
"*Si, Signore.*"

"Why are you pouring it out of those big cans?"

"Lentini always brings the olive oil in these big cans. Then I pour it into the store bottles. Usually, he waits for me to empty the cans. But last time, you frightened him, so he ran away and left them. I pour off what I need every day."

I staggered back. Filomena looked pained. *"Che cosa, Signor* Gren? Have I done something wrong?"

"No—no—nothing, Filomena."

I sprinted down the steps, down the dirt road, through the town, to the beach, where I found my wife stuffing soggy pizza into our children.

"Do you know what that dumb flatfoot has been carrying our oil in?" I gasped. "In oil cans!"

"It's oil, isn't it?"

"Hilarious," I yelled—awakening a dozen fat *borghese* from their mid-day snoozes. "Esso cans! Motor oil! Marfak! Havoline! Essolube! For God's sake, woman, I'm a stockholder in Standard Oil of New Jersey—but this is outrageous! And they're those big square cans with the little hole in the top! You ever try to clean out the *inside* of one of those? Impossible. We have been frying our veal in Mobiloil! Tossing salads with Veedol! You remember what happened in Morocco? All those people getting sick from drinking oil that was laced with airplane lubricants? I'll murder that sneaky cop—I'll make him drink his own poison!"

"Did Filomena say he always brings the oil in those cans?"

"Always! What a joke! He swears the oil is pure—no horse fat—and maybe he's telling the truth. But what does he carry it in? Motor oil cans!"

It is painful to report that my wife had been effectively Italianated. She made a helpless gesture with her hands. *"Caro,"* she said, "we have been using the oil from those cans for almost

121

two months. How sick can we get, if we haven't all died by now? Why aggravate yourself? You can't get the best of Italy. It's been here too long."

And so we went on, poisoning ourselves slowly with small doses of Esso Motor Oil. SAE 20, I believe it was. My surrender to Angelo Lentini was symbolic, I suppose. It had taken them about four months to defeat me, but they had succeeded. That is the great talent of Italy, and all praise to her. For all the alleged unsanitation in the country, they are a hearteningly healthy people—strong teeth, good bones, hardly any coronaries.

The following summer I witnessed another American succumb to Italian logic—that logic which frowns at mule fat in the olive oil, but will deliver the pure oil in a lubricant can. An American actor's wife, our neighbor at a beach near Rome, began to worry whether the local milk was pasteurized. In Rome proper, she knew, her children were drinking true pasteurized milk. (This reflects the presence of 15,000 permanent American residents there. Italians regard milk as semi-toxic, vaguely allied to body wastes, and fit only for the dying.)

The American lady spent three weeks seeking a straight answer about the local milk. The milkman swore on his mother's grave that it was. The grocer, his rival, said it was not, winking: "The milkman is the biggest liar in town." An Italian contessa advised the Americana that the milk was "purified but not pasteurized." Driven to rash acts, the lady tracked down the dairy. The manager greeted her warmly and took her on a guided tour. It was one of those huge Federconsorzi—a syndicate of big producers. She toured the plant. It was spotless, modern—and the milk was indeed pasteurized.

In the bottling plant, she saw the milk being poured into sparkling bottles.

122

"How do you wash these?" she asked.

"With the local water—from the wells," said the manager.

At this point, the American lady fainted. The local wells, as she had observed in her own bathroom and kitchen, pumped up water of a devious yellow-brown. Residents of the resort—and they included Italian millionaires, film celebrities and rich Americans—were warned against drinking it or even cooking with it. A bath in the local water left one smelling like a sulfur mine. It was fit only for scrubbing floors. One lived on bottled water. Yet the well water was being used to wash milk bottles!

Pasteurized milk—dirty bottles. Pure olive oil—carried in Motor Oil cans. My wife had the right idea. So long as no one got sick—why fight it?

To mix nationalities, the yang and yin of Italy will forever destroy our stubborn antiseptic logic.

CHAPTER ten

the great curve of life

An Italian's day is built around his midday meal. One may describe the daily routine in Italy as a curve, starting at a low point on the graph, when he awakens and eats a humble breakfast of strong coffee and hard bread. The curve begins a laborious ascent as he travels to work on bus, bike or foot and starts working. (Contrary to northern European prejudice, the Italian is a splendid worker—particularly the lower classes.) At 1:00 pm, Giovanni stops for his big meal. The curve ascends almost vertically, to a dizzy height, as all labor halts that the stomach may be appeased. There is a levelling off at mealtime, then a slow, delicious descent.

124

The midday meal is an event, a feast, a celebration of the partaker's membership among the living. It is a reminder that he has survived one more day, thumbing his nose at a harsh social system, a cynical government, an army of petty officials gone mad with the power of red tape, a barren land, a cruel history, and an oligarchy that never seems to learn. Whether our eater be a dock worker in Genoa, a clerk in Milan, or a ceramics artisan in Salerno, he sits down, almost always at home with his family, and lovingly works his way through six or seven dishes.

First, he honors the inevitable *pasta*. All the silly jokes about the amounts of spaghetti and allied products consumed by the Italians are true. And Italians should not be annoyed by these *droleries*—their pasta is superb. Tasty, filling, of noble texture, it lines the stomach with a soft, digestible bed on which can then rest a bit of fried meat, a pungent vegetable—chicory, spinach, escarole—a salad, a smidgin of cheese, an artfully peeled and sectioned peach, and lots of hard-crusted, nutritious bread.

All of this is gently washed in a mild alcoholic bath of wine, never enough to induce drunkenness (there is no such thing as a drunken Italian) but sufficient to render Giovanni and spouse drowsy, at ease with his precarious, limited life, tolerant of his exploiters. There is a marvelous stateliness to the midday meal, no matter how poor the diner. The curve of life reaches its peak, probably when the last of the lasagna is consumed, since the quality of the food generally declines thereafter. And so far as the great mass of Italians are concerned, they will not eat again that day. Only the rich eat a second meal—and that late at night, at a restaurant.

With the abdominal cavity now stretched to capacity, Giovanni undresses and retires to the matrimonial bed. Shutters are drawn—those slatted, impenetrable blinds that convert the brightest tropical daylight into a cave blacker and colder than a Sicilian landlord's heart. Husband and wife bed down—engorged, yawning, sated, gassy, as calm as altered cats, but with more potentialities.

The curve of life begins a slow, pleasurable slide. There are sighs, soughs, grunts, rest, sleep—a Mediterranean peace. Perhaps there is a visit from Eros. Minds are emptied. The digestive apparatus works rhythmically, absorbing the huge lump of healthful carbohydrate. The sun descends. At about 3:30 or 4:00, the shutters are raised with startling clatter—and the curve takes a headlong plunge. Work must be resumed.

Back they trek to factories, offices and shops—but their minds and hearts are elsewhere. Big shots do not get to their desks until 5:00 or later. Government functionaries may not show up until 6:00. And the entire country stumbles along in a torpid slow-motion.

Stand before the desk of a minor official—a police investigator, a customs inspector—and you will be an aggrieved witness to the great afternoon half-sleep of Italy. No matter how good your Italian or short your temper, he will hear only a third of what you say. One eye closes; he responds in monosyllables. He will suffocate a winey belch, scratch himself, lower his head, hum the latest Modugno hit. The day is dying, and so is he. The curve of life is falling, ever falling, and existence is reaching its nadir. At 7:30, when the workday is over, the curve will bottom out and dribble off. There may be a slight, erratic rise when he watches television later, but life long ago reached its orgiastic summit—with the *ziti alla bolognese*. Like Scott Fitzgerald's life after Princeton, everything after the pasta is anticlimax.

These musings lead me to the matter of Italians on vacation. And what I say now must concern largely the middle and upper

classes—my beloved *borghese*. The main concern of a vacationing Italian is to sharpen the rise of the curve, that is, to eat and
sleep much more than he normally does in the midday period.
The meal is twice as long and a bit more elegant. The hours of
slumber are extended to 5:30 or 6:00. Only the morning is
utilized for activities, and these consist mainly of sitting on a
hot pebbly beach, and dozing. By 1:00 pm only crazy Americans
linger at the seaside.

(I now hear a rising murmuration of professional Europe-
lovers, none of whom is more violent than an Italy-lover, chiding
me for my narrow intolerance. Let me hasten to explain that
these observations are made without value judgments. No objections are raised here to Italians eating and sleeping on their holiday. Maybe they have found something. Look at their low rate
of heart disease and mental illness.)

In Rapallo, we had ample opportunities to study the wealthy
Italian at ease, relaxed, vacationing. Our first observation was
that a holiday for an Italian is an occasion to *dress up,* instead of
down. At the midday ritual feeding in hotels and restaurants
(apart from the half-moon set who were largely single girls) the
borghese wear dark suits, stiff white collars and ties. Their ladies
appear in sedate dresses, corseted and high-heeled. The children
have the scrubbed, barbered look of Sunday school goers.

Vacations are formalized, sombre. No one plays tennis. Very
few go boating. No one fishes. The reasons relate to Italy's
stratified social structure. Remember that by and large only the
well-off take vacations. Time off from work is a time to reinforce
their status, their power. No one goes fishing because fishing is a
poor man's work. Along all the rugged Ligurian coastline, in
four months, I saw only three old men with poles in the water.
Similarly, picnics are abhorred. Eating in the countryside is a

127

peasant's stigma; even the most humble families will spend Sunday eating in a plain rustic *trattoría*, rather than eat on the grass.

As for the dazzling Italian landscape—and it is staggering in its variety and colors—it is apparently reserved for foreigners. It is difficult for me to recall a single instance of an Italian stopping his Fiat at a lookout point, or a clearing, to observe the grand sweep of a rocky coastline, or a mighty mountain range. Swedes, Germans, English, Americans—the visitors will breathe in the magic compositions of intense blue sky, black cypresses, green pines, gray rocks and turquoise waters—but Italians happily ignore them.

It is not sufficient to say they are used to them, and hence snub the natural wonders. They simply don't care. Twenty-five hundred years of bad leadership have convinced them that all that really matters is enough food, and a safe niche in the social system. If you are poor, you worry about eating, a job, and your family. If you are rich, you are concerned about eating, your family, and the maintenance of *la bella figura*—a good front to show the world. And if you are a *borghese*, that front is ill-served by wearing casual clothes (the way wealthy Americans do) or fishing (a lowly occupation) or gazing at a sunset (it is worth nothing in lire).

During our last two weeks at the Casa Stoppani Marie and I clashed violently with the *borghese* syndrome. An Italian family from Milan rented Officer Lentini's apartment for the last half of August. The cop deposited his family with a sister in Santa Margherita, and the summer renters moved in.

Happily, I told Marie: "Thank goodness *Il Rompere-Coglioni* is gone. The guy has been driving me crazy. He's in the bedroom every morning, admiring the way I type. He says now he knows why I'm a *Professore*. I type so good. I have to get rid of him with a Swiss cigar, and I'm running out of them."

Fool that I am, I did not realize that a family of Milanese can be infinitely more wearing than a nosey Calabrian cop.

The father of the new tenanting group was addressed as *Dottore*. I was forever tempted to ask him to tape my ankle, or inspect the rash on David's bottom. Actually, he was a textile broker—but the *Dottore* was all his. He had graduated from high school. Like many northern Italians, he was tall, fair and long-headed—a solemn man, thoroughly aware of his eminence. His wife was also tall, darkly pretty, splendid in puffed-out coiffeur and wasp-waisted bouffant frocks. She favored a perpetual haughty simper. They had two small children, a boy and a girl, both under four. It was impossible to distinguish their sexes.

The children merit description. Both were dainty, spotless, fair-skinned little changelings, raised under glass, fed on faery dust. How they were kept so immaculate astounded me. One or both of the maids in the employ of *la famiglia* Nardulli was forever chasing them, scrubbing their faces, flicking dirt from their tender pink limbs, whitening their shoes, changing soiled socks and knitted white shirts and adorable white caps. They were not children. They were exhibits, pets, toys. I would look at our own three assassins—in ragged shorts, faded shirts, barefoot, layered with Italy's ancient earth—and marvel at cultural diversity. To keep Nancy, Teddy and David in that pristine state would have required a platoon of English nannies armed with police billies.

The Nardullis, as a group, were disturbingly cold and disdainful. We smiled, offered greetings in Italian, pretended to fuss over their changelings. In response, we would get an occasional stiff nod of their long heads. We soon abandoned efforts at cordiality. The Italian upper classes are wonderfully self-suffi-

129

cient. Throw away all those myths about happy, jolly, out-going Italians as far as the *borghese* are concerned—particularly northern *borghese*. They are as bland as Swiss grocers, and can be as surly as French provincial tax collectors. Rapallo was a city in this stone-faced tradition. I never saw anyone singing out of doors; any horseplay among the sexes; men chasing girls; girls chasing men; men chasing men. Teen-agers behaved with a quiet relentless stolidity, gathered about jukeboxes. Once a party of itinerant Neapolitans wandered along the Lungomare with a guitar, seeking to arouse the citizenry with song. The carabinieri warned them to shut up and keep moving.

Despite the Nardullis' refusal to grant us regonition, we soon found ourselves in extended negotiations with them. These proceedings arose out of two holiday habits of the Milanese family —the schedule they kept, and their footgear. I have already mentioned that a vacation to an Italian is an opportunity to steepen and raise the great curve of life, notably the sleeping and eating aspects. Let us examine the manner in which the Nardullis worked this.

They would rise early, the children at 6:00 or 6:30, the parents at about 7:30. Immediately—from the time the kids were up—there would be a deafening stomping above us, as the little faeries clattered across Lentini's sonorous marble floors, raising echoes and reverberations amid all that noise-producing stone, glass and hard plaster.

Oh, but it was not ordinary stomping. All members of the household—*Il Dottore*, his *Signora*, both *bambini*, and the two maids—wore *heavy wooden clogs*. I will go on record as stating that there is no louder, harsher, more penetrating, more shattering sound than that of six pairs of hard wooden shoes pounding on a marble floor over one's head at cock-crow. Often

I felt we were under an army of lunatic workmen with jack-hammers. One morning I dreamed that atomic fallout had raised a breed of giant woodpeckers, who were at work in the woods without.

The clogging and stomping went on, ceaseless, until about 9:00, when all but one maid, would pile into the family Lancia and depart for the beach. At 1:30 they were back, well burned, and the noises of both wooden shoes and heavy eating continued for an hour and a half.

Then the curtain of sleep would descend. Shutters were slammed. Utter silence would settle over the second floor of the Casa Stoppani, until 6:30 in the evening. Then all would rise and don formal attire—*Il Dottore* in a black suit, polished black pumps and a maroon tie; *La Signora* in a flouncy print frock and a new simper; the two little delicacies in puffy white starched clothes and virginal white high shoes; the two sullen maids in fresh cottons and high heels. Then the troupe would ride off in the Lancia, park it, and promenade along the Lungomare ten or twelve times, staring at the other vacationers. They would return at about 8:30 and watch television until 11:00—the children remaining awake. Then they would retire noisily, the kids awakening once more at 6:00 to bombard our weary heads with the explosions of their cursed wooden shoes.

How can I do justice to the nerve-racking impact of that noise? Under the best of conditions—let us say late afternoon, as I sat alone, trying to write, happy with an espresso and a Swiss cigar—the noise of those heels would set me trembling. In the early morning stillness, with Marie and myself searching for slumber like knights after a new lead on the Holy Grail, it was insufferable.

"Do something!" Marie said to me. "Go up there and tell

them they have no right to wear those wooden clogs in the morning!"

Ever since my humiliation by Frezzolini, I had preferred to avoid conflict with the *borghese*. They were too cunning for me. They were too cunning for their own good, I suspect, and will suffer for it some day—but that is their worry.

"If you don't, I will," Marie said. The threat stirred me. My wife loses all refinements in front of the upper class Italian. She becomes violently aware of her own antecedents in Salerno—people who did the laundry and cooking for the likes of the Nardullis—and allows these old blood ties to color her dialogue.

That morning I trapped Nardulli as he was leading his brood to the Lancia. *"Mi scusi, gentile Dottore,"* I began politely. "But those wooden shoes you and your esteemed family wear in the morning, they make a terrible loud noise on the marble floor. My wife and I cannot sleep."

The clogs came to parade rest on the terrazzo steps. "What do you wish to tell me?" Nardulli asked, unsmiling.

"Excuse me, *Dottore,* but I have just told you. You and your adorable family insist on wearing those hard wooden shoes. The noise in our apartment below is unbearable."

Nardulli looked away from me at his beautiful wife. She brushed back a few strands of hair the color of root beer. The brace of maids fussed and fidgeted around the little boy and the little girl, dusting dirt from a sweater, dabbing at a white shoe with a handkerchief.

"He says we wear wooden shoes," Nardulli told his *Signora.* "Naturally, he would not understand."

"What don't I understand?" I asked.

Il Dottore smiled—ever so faintly. "Wooden shoes—*zoccoli*—are what one is *supposed* to wear at the beach."

132

"Ah yes," I said, feeling faint, seeing already an imminent defeat. "But when people below you are trying to sleep, and when there are marble floors, perhaps courtesy might dictate that one removes the wooden shoes, and goes about in socks or in soft shoes."

His wife snickered. I knew what was amusing her. Only a boorish American would dream of people of status, *la famiglia* Nardulli, walking around their vacation home in stockings!

"When else can one wear *zoccoli*?" asked Nardulli, as if conducting a lesson. "Such shoes are made only for the beach. I spend my entire year working hard in Milan, that I may enjoy the freedom of *zoccoli* for two weeks in Rapallo. Would you deny me this pleasure?"

"No sir, I would not. Would you deny me my sleep?"

"Why must one sleep so late in the morning?" Nardulli asked, with evident disgust at my barbaric American ways.

"Our customs are different than yours, *Dottore*. We like to sleep late. As late as 8:00 in the morning sometimes. Oh, if I could truthfully describe to you the horrid clatter and banging of those six pairs of wooden shoes! And how fast your beautiful little children run! And when those two diligent maids try to catch them! The noise deafens me and makes me tremble."

The simperer had had enough of *me*. She tugged at her husband's sleeve, and off they clopped. Not a promise had been given me, no sympathy, understanding, consideration. Of course, I had learned the word for wooden shoes—*zoccoli*. And by god, one wore *zoccoli* at a beach resort, and *zoccoli* they would wear, from rosy-fingered dawn to beddy-bye. His Milanese logic almost moved me—I saw him sitting in his stuffy office all year, waiting for those two weeks in Rapallo when he could wear wooden shoes, sleep sixteen hours a day, and engorge his peritoneum.

For a few more mornings we lay awake, shuddering at the horrid clangor above us, the inevitable 6:00 alarum. In fact, we would awaken well before 6:00, in anticipation of it. For little tykes, they could really run—and the sour-faced maids were no slouches either. Marie could bear it no longer.

"Coward!" she cried. "I've had enough of those clowns! If you won't face up to them, I will!"

In pink baby doll, she vaulted from the bed and raced out. She is a fast runner and has a drawerful of old Police Athletic League medals for Girls' 40 yard dash to prove it. She made it upstairs in a few seconds. I staggered after her in my shorties, pleading for prudence.

"Marie—sweetheart!" I yelled. "Don't do anything rash! They're an ally! Nardulli is probably a big wheel in the Christian Democrats! You insult him and we'll have to give up the missile bases!"

But already she had flown into the apartment, and was blasting.

"*Per piacere! Per carità!*" my wife screamed. "Please! Have mercy! I beg you! Can't you people consider someone else? I know you're supposed to wear wooden shoes at the beach. But *San Giuseppe!* Not when other people are trying to sleep! Not at 6:00 in the morning!"

Nardulli, in hastily donned silk dressing gown, viewed her with high contempt. "*Signora* you are *mal'educata*. You have no right to intrude like this. No wonder the world is distrustful of you Americans. Oh, we are aware of you. Yes, you are rich and powerful, but as is well known, you have no manners."

"Manners!" Marie shouted. "At least we take off our wooden shoes in the house!"

At that moment, the infant changelings, all pink and white

134

and tender, clattered into the room, clack-clack-clacking on their *zoccoli,* followed by both maids, similarly shod in hard wood.

"Listen to it," Marie moaned. "Just listen. It's even louder down where we are."

For a moment I thought my wife had surrendered—one more victory for the *borghese.* But at the doorway, she turned. (Coward that I was, I had stayed in the corridor.)

"I warn you, *Dottore,*" Marie said. "You had better stop wearing *zoccoli* in the morning. If you insist on wearing them, do you know what I shall do?"

"You can do nothing," Nardulli said. His voice was edged with fear.

"Hah! Don't be so sure! Every afternoon, *Dottore,* I know that you and your family go to sleep for four hours. As soon as I hear the shutters go down, I will stand under your bedroom window on our balcony and play our three American radios very loud. I will rent a piano and play it. I will hire bands of roving musicians to make noise. I will invent noisy games for my children, games in which they scream at one another. And you and your *Signora,* and your children, and the maids will sleep no more. Think of it, *Dottore*—noise, noise, ugly noise, when you are trying to sleep in the afternoon."

She had stabbed him—a very palpable hit.

"I—I will call the police," Nardulli said, outraged.

"That will do no good. The Rapallese police are notoriously generous to *Americani.* My husband has given them large sums of money, and is on friendly terms with the Chief. He is the Marshall Plan of the Rapallo police. They will not help you."

These lies had their effect. As Nardulli sank into a sofa, I could see his *Signora,* emerging from the bedroom in a cloud of pale blue chiffon, tossing her puffy hair. She almost seemed agitated, as if Marie's furious assault had at long last produced some reaction in that fleshy, self-indulgent island of ego.

My wife's outrageous attack produced results. Early morning zoccoli-wearing ended. Where all of my quiet diplomacy had failed, her big mouth had succeeded. Threats, intrigue, prevarications—these had whipped the wooden shoe brigade into line. Her brinkmanship had succeeded where my rational dialogue had flopped—as rationalism always will before the Nardullis of the world.

Then, at 12:30 one cool August morning, the calm along the *Che Puzza* River was shattered—not by *zoccoli*, but by a variety of screams, shouts and curses. We tried to ignore it, but the noise got louder. Soon we heard one pair of wooden heels clattering down the stairs. There followed an infernal pounding on our door, the sound of a woman weeping.

Marie and I sprung from our bed of pain—Stoppani's *letto matrimoniale* consisted of a thin hard wire net, ridged down the middle, and helped explain Liguria's low birth rate. We ran to the corridor where we found our maid Filomena comforting one of Nardulli's indentured servants. This one doubled as cook—a tiny, homely girl, no more than 19. She was crying painfully, was dressed in a blue suit, wore her high wooden heels, and carried a cardboard valise.

"*Poverina*, poor little thing," Filomena said. "Those terrible people upstairs have thrown her out in the middle of the night! Without salary! Without her pension book, or her hospitalization stamps! Nothing!"

We took the little cook into our living room and tried to stop her sobbing. Marie fed her a Miltown and glass of *aqua minerale*, and her weeping subsided.

She told us the sad story. That evening, they had discovered

136

that one of the hinges on Lentini's refrigerator was broken—mangled beyond repair. A new hinge was needed. *Il Dottore* Nardulli at once accused her of breaking it. She was the cook; ergo, she had broken it. The little cook, in turn, blamed the children. (Although my sentiments were with the cook, I kept an open mind on the matter of guilt. Italian domestics traditionally accuse *i bambini*. I have *seen* a cook smash a bowl and then grin at me: "*I bambini* broke it").

The argument had waxed violent, and Nardulli threatened to slap her—a crime beyond the pale of civilized behavior in Italy, a country addicted to a lot of yelling, but no hitting. She had threatened Nardulli with the enforcement powers of her union, her family and the police, and the bitterness mounted. Finally, in a burst of rage, *Il Dottore* ordered her out of the house—in the middle of the night, without the money due her, with no way of getting home. She told us she had a brother in Genoa, and if we telephoned him, he would come on his Vespa for her.

"Ah, the good old Italian *borghese*," I said. "If we dared to treat our help like that, we'd be the fat, rich, nasty Americans. But there are no ethical problems involved for an Italian employer—anything goes, and his serfs accept it."

Filomena thoughtfully translated my comments for the cook. The little girl absorbed it, then shook her head. "Oh no, *Signor* Gren. It is not *Il Dottore's* fault. It is your fault, your wife's fault that all this happened."

"Ours?" I asked—preparing myself for one more insight into the Latin mind.

"Yes. Everything was happy upstairs until you made us stop wearing our *zoccoli*. One goes to the beach to wear *zoccoli*. And when you forced us to take them off, everyone became angry and nervous. The children would not eat. *La Signora* forgot to

137

go to the beauty parlor one day. The refrigerator broke. And *Il Dottore* was so upset he chased me out of the house. I cannot help saying this, *Signor* Gren. But all this misery is because of what you did to us."

What *we* did. All we had wanted was our sleep, some surcease from that earsplitting rat-a-tat-tat above us every dawn. And now we had ruined the happiness of the Nardulli household.

Filomena telephoned the cook's brother in Genoa. An hour later he came blasting up the dirt road on his Vespa, to bear her back to the bosom of her family. Still sniffling, she seemed to bear no real grievance against *Il Dottore*. Italian domestics take for granted the orneriness of Italian employers. The real villains of the piece, she had made clear to me, were the crazy Americans —*La Famiglia Gren*—who had forced on them a change of folkways, and had thus brought on misery. I suspect there is a lesson here for our foreign aid program, but I am not prepared to pursue it all the way.

The little cook left. She offered no thanks for the Miltown, the *aqua minerale,* the comforting words, the use of our phone. Nothing—no amount of Point Four or Peace Corps assistance could make up for our rude abrogation of the *zoccoli* tradition. There is, apparently, nothing worse than a *zoccoli*-scoffer.

A few days later I saw *Il Dottore* Nardulli, back from his morning at beach, ready for his two hour lunch and four hour snooze. On the steps of the Casa Stoppani, he was intercepted by an official looking gent in a baggy suit, carrying an enormous briefcase. They became engaged in great argument—wild gestures, shouts, threats. I pretended to be engrossed in my Rome *Daily American.*

The caller was an official of the domestics' syndicate in Genoa, and he had come to claim the cook's back pay, her pension book, her hospitalization stamps, and to advise the doctor that he was liable to several fines and penalties for his precipitate action.

The official left. Nardulli, clutching a fistful of documents that explained to him his malfeasances and the punishments to be visited on him, clop-clopped up the steps. He spied me reading and halted.

"So—I hope you are now satisfied," he said bitterly. "You are without culture or education. To ruin a man's vacation in that manner—that is not the sign of a civilized person. But what else can one expect from Americans?"

In a sense he was right. I *had* ruined his vacation. Sleeping, eating, the perpetual wearing of wooden shoes—these were the joys of an Italian holiday, the sharpening of the rise of the great curve of life. For a while, I toyed with the notion of letting him put on his *zoccoli* in the mornings and clatter around above me. But my heart remained stoney. It had been my only triumph over the stolid *borghese*. Although I am a bad winner, one who regrets his victories, I am not *that* bad.

CHAPTER eleven

the Maestro

Alberto Moravia, in one of his novels, has a superbly perceptive passage about the art of motion picture writing. I find Moravia at his best when he is discussing matters *other* than sex —matters which represent a fragment of his work. Were the great Italian novelist to write a book in which there were no affairs, assignations, sexual debasements, and perhaps discuss the annual rainfall in the Po Valley, or the manufacture of straw chairs in Chiavari, he would write a classic. But all we get is bed, bed, bed.

Regarding screen writing, Moravia notes that there are certain motion pictures which are obviously doomed from the day they start—and everyone concerned knows it. The producer secretly knows it. The director knows it. Above all, the writer knows it, and he knows it from the moment the book, or play, or treatment from which he is to fashion a screenplay, is given to him. Yet all involved observe the ritual—the agonized appraisals, the endless meetings, the arguments, the technical discussions of trivia—fully aware that not a frame of film will ever be shot.

When I read the passage, I jumped and cheered the novelist out loud. Such perceptions are admirable; Moravia had pinpointed a recurrent aspect of movie writing—notably movie writing in Italy. During our Rapallo sojourn, I worked for a month on an Italian film, and I experienced to the last FADE OUT, the mechanics of what I shall call *Moravia's Law*.

I had asked my agent in Rome—a branch of the Music Corporation of America, known as MCA, or The Octopus—to see about a movie job for me. The young Italian attorney in charge of the office felt it was unlikely—there was a glut of American and English writers in Italy, and besides, I had only one screen credit. Then, a fortuitous coincidence put me to work.

A well-known Italian director, one Marcello Piselli, was going to spend most of July at a villa in Santa Margherita, the town between Rapallo and Portofino. Piselli had been assigned a project by a famous Roman movie producer, and the director needed an American writer to help him "polish" a screenplay they already had. The pay was not excessive, but the experience promised to be a rich one. Besides, after the manner in which Frezzolini had bled me, I felt the urge to fatten the bank account.

Comforting myself with Dr. Johnson's wisdom (No man but a blockhead ever wrote for anything except money) I accepted, and awaited the arrival of the Great Piselli.

Arrive he did, with entourage. The trailing entourage is characteristic of most artistic Italians; perhaps we should copy the idea. The aforementioned Signor Moravia may often be seen strolling down the Via Veneto or at the resort of Fregene, followed by a school of noisy pilot fish—literary critics, lesser writers, essayists, journalists, fringe movie people, and an occasional foreign writer, hoping for a kind word. (These words are written out of a certain unbecoming jealousy. I once introduced myself to Moravia on the Veneto, citing as mutual friends, some people at my Milanese publishing house, who had told me they were close to him. He shrugged and turned his back on me.)

In Piselli's case, the entourage was an all-girl affair. He arrived in Santa Margherita with a wife, two daughters, a secretary, and the woman who was to be the art director on our foredoomed undertaking. I often thought of Piselli as a great floating island, surrounded by little female islets.

The director greeted me effusively on the balcony of his modest pink villa. He was not a rich man. Unlike American directors of the top rank, who are paid enough money to clean a block of Philadelphia slums, Italian directors have to scratch for what they can get. But his uninflated income did not reduce his enthusiasms. Piselli hugged me, kissed me, punched me in the small of the back, and offered me Coca-Cola. The refreshment was no attempt to patronize me; he liked Coca-Cola.

"*Signor* Gren!" he boomed. "You and I—I can see we are *simpàtico!* We will write a great, great movie together! The script I have here needs a few changes, some shortening, some development of character! In four weeks, we will do a magnificent job!"

His voice boomed and exploded; it was an actor's voice. I liked him immediately. He appeared to be about 45, and I was stunned to learn from his secretary, a shrewd Venetian lady named Lucia Calmo, that he was 57! He was above average in height for an Italian male, barrel-chested, handsome, clean-shaven, with bushy sandy hair, rising in Groucho-like peaks, and a pair of alert, popping green eyes. What enamored me to him was his outrageous, ribald, Rabelaisian view of life. Here was no stiff-necked, silent *borghese*—Piselli was Renaissance man and show biz, a formidable amalgam.

I can best illustrate his lovable character by his analysis of our task at our first script conference. With loud quavering voice, with vigorous gestures, he summed up his sentiments about the screenplay:

"My dear Gren—this is a story of *faith!* Of a father's faith, a mother's faith, a daughter's faith! Of faith in Heaven and in God. A story of beauty—and life—and the sorrow of death. Of the eternal truths all of us live by. And that is why I love this story. Ah—but will it make customers pay to see the film?"

"Yes," I answered, "if you are that enthusiastic about it."

"No!" Piselli shouted. "Not faith!"

"Well—we will write it so well that—"

"No! Guess again—why will people pay to see our film?"

"It will have a superb cast of international stars—"

"Hah! Puppets! Talking birds! Again, Gren, guess!"

"I give up Maestro, what?" Already, I had learned to call him Maestro.

The Great Piselli clapped one huge freckled hand over his crotch and shouted: "This! *Sexy!*"

How could I help but admire such frankness about the motion picture industry? The word *sexy* incidentally, is the same in Italian—a free adaptation of the English—and it has a peculiarly innocent, ludicrous sound when shouted by an Italian.

143

Lucia Calmo, his assistant secretary and interpreter, became my own confidante and informer. She was a thin, severely attractive woman with black hair worn tight on her head, with a bun in the back, dangly gold ear-rings, and winking gold teeth. Like most Venetians, she was cynical, shrewd and intelligent. She was divorced and spoke very little about herself—but on the subject of Maestro Marcello Piselli, she was a mother lode of anecdotes.

"He should be up there with the greatest of Italian directors," she told me. "Rossellini, DeSica, Blassetti—they have nothing on him. But he is like a child. He gets into ridiculous arguments over trivia. He holds grudges. He refuses to speak to a certain actor, a cameraman, a member of the crew, over some imagined insult. The producers are afraid to hire him."

I liked him better every minute. Lucia told me that Piselli would appear on the set in riding breeches, sun-helmet and boots, flicking a fly-whisk—and no one dared snicker at him. He had a quick temper and hard fists. Producers and assorted money-lenders stayed away when he directed. Once he had seized a producer's flunky and stuffed him into a trash barrel.

That night I took home a pile of material to read. There was an English translation of the original novel, which was the basis of the film. There was also the first Italian screenplay, and a literal English translation of that screenplay.

When I had struggled through all three, well past midnight, I realized the impossible mission confronting us. The prospect was depressing, and had I not found Maestro Piselli's company so intriguing, and were I not greedy, I would have backed out.

The material was fascinating, in a horrid kind of way. The original novel had been written in Icelandic, and was set in Iceland. Later, it had appeared as Italian paper-bound, which had

144

attracted the big producer. The story was a variety of Nordic Eugene O'Neill—a fogbound, brooding, bloodstained melodrama. There was a hardfisted old father, a kind of Keflavik Big Daddy, a rebellious son, a suffering mother, and a mysterious daughter, as strange as she is beautiful. Actually, she was the bastard child of an American paratroop officer and the local lady of the evening. (I gathered that the fancy lady, since deceased, had not been too bad a sort. She only worked at nights, and the nights were short way up there near the Arctic Circle).

The plot suffered from an abundance of incident. Under a heavy fog, on the bleak, treeless landscape, the characters indulged in murder, incest, suicide and cheating at dominoes. Everything was conducted in a stoic, grunting Nordic frigidity.

As I concluded my reading of the novel, in the dim light of Casa Stoppani, as the *Che Puzza* River gurgled by with its nightly burden of refuse, I turned to the English translation of the screenplay—on which several notable Italian writers had labored. An international crime was evident. The misty northern air had been transmuted into a wild, screaming, Latin atmosphere. Everyone yelled. People made impassioned speeches. Rhetoric had replaced reticence. Women clutched at their hearts and fell into dead faints. Men swore blood vengeance, biting their thumbs. The Italian writers had left us with the damnedest collection of Latinized Icelanders—a frozen tundra in Naples.

Herewith is a sampling of the literal English translation of the screenplay:

TORS. So. You. My only beloved son! Betraying our blood! You are repulsive!

SVEN. I? Repulsive? You, old man, you are horrid—toad!

TORS. You dare call me toad? Blood of my blood! You stink of crime and debased activities! Cretin!

SVEN. (*screaming, as he picks up a pitchfork*) You hear that, Mama? Are you witness to these sarcastic things that Papa says to me? Ah, Mama, by all the Saints and the Virgin, do more than nod your head with sorrow when he abuses me like that! I am—your son!

TORS. (*also screaming*) Put down the pitchfork, imbecile. I will teach you once and for all to call old Tors Torsbjorn a toad! Moron! Donkey! I will grind you into fertilizer!

(*Sven advances on Tors with the pitchfork. Tors picks up a rake. They circle each other. Ingrid screams as they strike at one another; blood flows from a wound on Tor's arm, but he laughs insanely*).

Why go on? There were 145 pages of this, concluding with a storm at sea. Moravia's Law was operating. Doom stared me in the face—and I could not back out.

The next morning I went bravely to Piselli's pink villa in Santa Margherita. Beneath a pleasant grape arbor, sipping Coca-Cola, the Maestro asked me for my opinions of the novel and the screenplay. Hypocrisy, I have always felt, is not the worst of sins in motion picture work. My limited hoard of integrity is preserved for books and documentary work.

"It is fascinating, Maestro," I began—truthfully.

"*Affascinante*," Lucia translated.

"Exactly what I feel!" Piselli shouted. "I am so glad you see it my way! *Caro* Gren! I knew, you and I were *simpàtico!*"

He hugged me, resumed his seat—a canvas director's chair he had brought up from Rome—and launched a half hour lecture on his notions of the film. There would be very little dialogue. All would be suggested in visual imagery. People would express entire pages of words—in the current script—with grimaces and gestures. And above all, we would write a story of *faith*.

146

Faith? I wondered. Whose? The characters did nothing but scream at one another, before resorting to more hurtful modes of assault. But I did not interrupt Piselli. I enjoyed his peroration, which, I realized was in accord with all directors' speeches to writers. Translated, these speeches would read as follows:

"I am the director, and you are the writer, and although you are a bright fellow and I like you, never forget that I am far more important than you, that I am in charge, and the junk you write will mean nothing to me, absolutely nothing, because even if you defy me, which is unlikely if you want to get paid, I will do the film my own way, when you have departed."

Again, I realize, the bonds of trade were much firmer than any linkage based on national traits. Piselli was blood brother to the movie directors of the world—American, English, Swedish. To the Lentinis and Frezzolinis of his fatherland he would always be a stranger.

He appeared to be just getting wound up—his bushy sandy hair breeze-stirred, his jellied green eyes darting and rolling. But suddenly Lucia Calmo stood up, yawned and announced she wanted to go swimming—she was tired of hearing the same old stuff. Surprisingly, Piselli obeyed her—after cursing her liberally. But first, he wished to hear my opinions of the screenplay— what changes I would recommend, what additions I envisioned. The bald truth was, I had no opinions. The film could never be made. But I owed Piselli something; and the producer *was* paying me, so I was obliged to contribute.

I began cautiously.

"*Allora,* perhaps we should study the heavy, tragic nature of this story. True, it is a melodrama. A melodrama about peasants —dull, heavy people. But I am fearful if we maintain that

147

atmosphere for an hour and three-quarters, people will fall asleep and will advise other people to stay away from our film."

I had been speaking in what I fancied to be rather good, if slow, Italian—about half the speed at which Piselli spoke. The Maestro had been slumped in his canvas chair, like a Roman pro-consul sent to suppress an uprising of fierce Ligurian tribes of the coast. Impatiently, as I made my case, he rolled his lime-colored eyeballs, losing them, so that all I saw were the blood-shot whites. At the mention of people staying away from our movie, he sat upright and pointed from me to Lucia.

"Gren," he commanded. "Spik Anglish."

Gren, reprimanded for his plodding Italian, spikked Anglish. I went on to tell Piselli that the film lacked humor. Cautiously, I advanced the argument that rustic people had a capacity for earthy laughter, that all that close association with animals, witnessing the digestive and reproductive functions, endowed them with a ribald barnyard wit, and that the only way we could rescue the movie from being a gloomy failure, with Latinized Icelanders screaming murder, would be to spice it with some natural laughs. I made clear to Piselli that I didn't want one-line gags, but believable comic situations which would relate to the plot and to the characters.

Piselli slumped again in his chair of office. Then he leaped to his espadrilled feet—he was the most agile, vigorous 57-year old man I have ever seen—and shouted: "Humor! Yes! Jokes! Gren —you are a genius! That is exactly what is missing! Oh, Gren, you and I will make this a great comedy! Sexy! Box office!"

For a moment I suspected that the Maestro shared my sense of inevitable collapse. He had risen too quickly to my bait. Actually, I had made the suggestion because it was all I could think of—and Piselli had clutched it to his stout bosom with a

148

fierce delight that betrayed an uneasiness on his part with the assignment.

And so to work. First we wrote an outline. The patient Lucia sat between us translating faster than any United Nations professional. Then we proceeded to the script, still utilizing Lucia as go-between. (I am still annoyed with Piselli's intolerance of my Italian. As soon as I would embark on a well-constructed speech, rehearsed the night before with Filomena, he would hold up his consular hand and shut me up with: *Spik Anglish*).

And, oh, the humor we larded that screenplay with!

Old Tors, the tyrannical father emerged as a kind of Icelandic Red Skelton. He did pratfalls, tripping over the plow; was hit by crumbling chimneys; got kicked by a mule; dogs used his boots as handy substitutes for tree trunks. Piselli would roar with laughter as he thought up new ways to inject laughter into our weighty Nordic saga. How he danced around the garden, the day he decided that Tors, bending to strike Sven with a whip, had his pants split up the back!

Nothing in the original screenplay was spared my modest suggestion. The young lovers, at work in a hayrick, were attacked by swarms of gnats. Mama Torsbjorn, knitting by the fire (we had her knitting so much she could have furnished mufflers for the enlisted personnel of the 29th division) would hit the cottage floor as her rocker fell apart.

We had created an Icelandic Laff-Riot—Nordic Eugene O'Neill reincarnated as Latin Marx Brothers. Let me quote a sample from the new screenplay—a monster born of Gren's sly suggestion, and Piselli's enthusiasms.

TORS. (*belches loudly*) Where is that boy Sven? Sven, come help me with the hay!

(*Sven sneaks into the barn behind Tors, grinning. He signals to Jan and Karl, who sneak in with him. All three crawl on hands and knees toward the bellowing figure of old Tors. Then, they stealthily drop a string of lighted firecrackers between his legs.*)

TORS. (*belching*) Where are you, you young ruffian? I'll tan your no-good hide!

(*Tors spins around and espies the three boys sulking off. Just then the firecrackers explode. Tors does a wild comical dance, brandishing his pitchfork.*)

TORS. Yaaah! Yaaah! Villains! To do this to the old man!

(*The boys cackle and hoot at him and race out. Sven trips on a bucket of water, Jan and Karl trip on him. The goat breaks loose and butts Sven in the behind.*

Firecrackers keep exploding and set fire to the hay. Fire roars and snaps through the barn. The boys get up, but are blinded by the smoke and fall into a manure pile.

Tors, also blinded, jabs around wildly with his pitchfork. He pokes it by mistake into a horse, who neighs, kicks his way out the stall, and runs off. The fire roars.)

TORS. Rascals! Come out! I'll teach you to play tricks on the old man!

As I look back on this creation, I am almost sorry it never reached the screen. We might have been evolving a new art form—and been unaware of it. One night, after a tough translating session with the wonderfully patient Lucia, I began jotting down the various permutations our screenplay had undergone since that poor Icelandic Hemingway had burst into print. Observe:

1. Original novel in Icelandic.
2. Italian translation: a paper-back with sexy cover.
3. First Italian screenplay, by a platoon of Italian writers.
4. Literal translation of said screenplay into English for my

benefit, containing such lines as: *Vile boy, who would lay dirty hands on his undefiled sister! Pah!*

(Companion piece to this, but not a true permutation: Literal translation of the Italian *novel,* for Gren's use.)

5. A combined Italian outline—result of long discussions at Piselli's villa, by Gren-Piselli-Lucia.

6. English translation of above.

7. English language screenplay, Gren's original, based on the outline and Piselli's prodding—Marx Brothers in Iceland. A potpourri of slapstick and ribaldry based on sexual and digestive functions, with hints of arson, incest and aggravated assault.

8. Lucia's translation of Gren's English screenplay, for Piselli —who spoke and read no English.

9. Piselli's lengthy Italian rewrite of Gren's screenplay.

10. Combined Lucia-Gren *retranslation* of Piselli's final official version, *back* to English.

Now we had two companion screenplays: Italian and English. The latter was the crucial one. It would be used by the Italian producer in Rome to entice some Hollywood studio or money-man into backing the venture. As the excerpt above indicates, only an unredeemed optimist could have held any hope of involving American dollars in this mishmash. But up to the last minute of defeat, Lucia told me later, Piselli, the producer, the producer's aides and hangers-on, were convinced they had a winner. They had the kind of faith that has sustained Italy through centuries of bad rulers and wrong decisions.

About a month later, I was urgently summoned to Rome for a crucial meeting. An important American film executive, an old-time producer of great wealth and power, was holding audiences in a suite at the Excelsior Hotel. Evidently, he was the last court of appeal for the property. The producer and Piselli wanted me there to add weight to their sales pitch—proof that an American had worked on the story, and was enthusiastic about it.

For two reasons—neither of which disturbed Piselli and the producer—I was a calculated risk. I had written only one screenplay, for a movie that was not a financial bonanza. Moreover, I do not possess the usual novelist's syndrome toward important Hollywood executives. There are two possible attitudes toward the moneyman. One is the flaunting of an intellectual contempt for these debasers of our cultural currency—the Ben Hecht technique. At the other extreme, is a bowing, scraping, flattering approach, in which the novelist-cum-scenarist makes favorable comparisons between their films and Kafka, asserts that movies are an *art form,* and congratulates the producer or studio head on his courage and good taste.

My reaction to studio executives, producers, and millionaire directors falls into neither of these categories. I feel sorry for them. I know that my pity is misplaced, but I cannot help it. I brim with sadness, worrying about the box office, their sons in military academies, their daughters in finishing schools, their hearts and kidneys, their savage battles with the New York accountants who run the industry. All this compassion on my part arises from my single Hollywood experience—a most pleasant one—and specifically, the executive dining table in the studio commissary.

What a sad table it was! It was very long, covered with gleaming silver and sparkling napery. Here and there were a variety of titillating, appetizing delicacies—half-sour pickles, crisp sauerkraut, ruby red peppers, wedges of aromatic cheese, salty crackers, onion crackers, black pumpernickel—yummy. But, stationed amid all these mouth-watering goodies was a fair sampling of the United States Pharmacopoeia. There were darkly menacing bottles of laxatives; polyethylene dispensers of liquid saccharin; vials of tranquilizers, ulcer soothers, digestive aids, carminatives, salt substitutes, multi-vitamin pills with added minerals, therapeutic dietary aids—a congeries of oral medications that betrayed a mass hypochondria based on television, falling box office receipts, and illiterate actors who demanded 50 per cent of the gross.

As I sat at the hired hands' end of the table, watching the stooped oldsters, these veterans of a great American industry, confront their unhappy pillboxes and bottles, I was overcome with a damp sadness. Their lunch-time was suggestive of an expensive old-folks' home—all those tasty titbits they had to eschew, all those laboratory concoctions they were obliged to chew. My heart went out to them—these sad, yellowing, white-haired tribal elders, discussing the odds on the fight at Olympic Stadium between a Mexican and a Negro, both with good digestion, or clacking gums over a colleague's financial disaster, or trading marginalia on some actor's abhorrent sex life.

It was there that I realized that these were Vanishing Americans, going the way of the passenger pigeon, the Micmac Indians and the general practitioner. My impressionable cardiovascular system bled for them. Never did I join in the nasty behind-the-hand comments of the younger laborers at the studio. Never did I blurt out unkind critiques about their bad grammar, their poor taste, their boorishness. No! It seemed to me they needed comforting, someone to tuck a blanket around their legs, to pat their heads, to assure them that television would go away tomorrow. My own meagre contribution to their well-being, the motion picture *The Last Angry Man,* hardly helped. It took more than a year to film and lost money.

It is my suspicion that the studio produced the film, because several of these elders, particularly the late Harry Cohn, were convinced that *they* were Dr. Samuel Abelman, my fictional physician—the outraged, moral, courageous, free-speaking slum Schweitzer. Indeed, Mr. Cohn, some months before his death, informed me that *The Last Angry Man* might have been written about him.

"I'm that fellah you wrote about," Mr. Cohn said. "I'm angry all right."

His revelation rather shook me. I knew, of course, that he did not read books himself. He depended on synopses, and had several court "readers." Still, his reaction stunned me. Mr. Cohn, according to a Los Angeles newspaper, left an estate worth $14,000,000—somewhat more than Sam Abelman was able to show when he died. All of this has cursed me with a recurrent nightmare. In it, I see Harry Cohn as a physician in a slum section of Brooklyn. He is climbing a flight of tenement stairs, carrying an old scuffed black satchel. The patient he is calling on is an aged Negro woman, dying of cancer of the colon.

Dr. Cohn administers to her, gives her an injection, makes her comfortable, assures her she will get better, and tells her to call him as soon as she feels pain again. The Negro woman mutters her thanks and asks him what his fee is.

Dr. Cohn replies:

"One million dollars and twenty-five per cent of the gross."

At this point, I wake up shivering and reach for the heating pad.

In sum, my one exposure to Hollywood has left me not with the routine novelists' contempt, which is expected of me, but with a profound sympathy for all those dyspeptic old champions, munching their creamalin and equanil. Thus, when Piselli and the producer summoned me to the Excelsior Hotel, to assist in

154

enticing the American movie king, I was of little help. Knowing in my heart-of-hearts that our slapstick melodrama was a lost cause, I was less than convincing in my narration.

The American, a small dandified man with a white pencil-line mustache and a beige suede vest, exuded that lost gloom I had come to associate with the Old Hands of filmdom. Obviously, he had not slept well, troubled with dreams of television sets. When I had concluded my synopsis of our epic, he made a few unpleasant comments in a bored, distant voice. The picture was a costume picture; it was downbeat; it had a foreign setting; nobody knew where Iceland was; no one in the audience could identify with anyone. I said nothing, because I agreed with him.

Piselli listened, seething, to Lucia's translations of the executive's bad review. I could see the Maestro's vigorous body writhing beneath his yellow silk suit; the brocade chair in which he sat seemed unable to hold him. The Italian producer noticed the furies seizing Piselli also, and made a movement toward him.

But Piselli was goaded into violence by the mogul's bland antagonism. Unlike me, the Maestro had faith—and he was a superb actor. As soon as the American had concluded, Piselli sprang from the chair, and in explosive Italian, laced with wild gestures, began to act out our sorry tale.

San Giuseppe, what a performance my hero gave! He was Tors, the old father—in a *basso profundo.* He was Sven, the mischievous son—in a tenor. He was the mysterious daughter—in falsetto. Piselli shouted, wept, laughed, screamed, and at one particularly emotion-charged moment, in a mad leap across the room, to illustrate a battle to the death between two drunken fishermen, he broke wind.

Stroking his tiny mustache, the natty little oldster watched him with noncommital eyes. He was not amused. As for the poor Italian producer, he kept shouting at Piselli to stop, but the Maestro was oblivious. Either that—or he knew darn well he wasn't getting across and decided to play it for laughs. I like to believe the latter was the case.

Now Piselli was squatting on the arm of a sofa—*crowing*. He flapped his arms, a perfect rooster, to signify a new dawn, the movie's last scene. There remained only the final embrace, as Sven and his putative sister (she wasn't really, remember?) find love at last. But for this climax a partner was needed; he would not solo.

His popping green eyes surveyed all present—and came to rest on the rich American's secretary. She was a German maiden lady, fluent in several languages, who apparently followed the money-man around Europe. I estimated her to be about six foot five, built along the lines of Wilt Chamberlain. Her hair was straw yellow and cut very short, and she was of that bony, prognathous breed of German woman who often supervised crematoria. She wore a brown tweed suit, orange hiking shoes, and a pince-nez on a black string. Piselli had elected her to share his ultimate ecstasy.

Jet-propelled, the Maestro bounded across the room and grabbed her with muscular arms.

"*Te amo; Te amo!* I love you! I love you!" Piselli murmured hotly in her antiseptic ear. "I don't care if you are my sister— you are not my sister!" His arms explored her wooden back, her long, fleshless flanks. She tried hard to shove him away—these German women are all ligament—but Piselli was having his own personal revenge for the Ardeatine massacre. He smothered her scrubbed, uncosmeticized face with wet Latin kisses. He gasped love spells in her ear. When she resisted, cursing him in polite

156

Italian, he only hugged tighter, looking up every now and then to the pale face of the old American, and asking: "Sexy? No?"

The second time he paused for critical approval—he never got it—she tried to escape him. He yanked her back, and both rolled from her chair to an ottoman, where Piselli shouted again:

"Now for the climax! She really loves him—although she has denied it all these years! She is more of a *putana* than he is, despite all her holiness!"

The German lady struggled once more. The ottoman was too small to hold them, and they hit the floor, just as a troop of Excelsior waiters, bearing espresso for all and a bottle of seltzer for the American, marched in. The waiters were all good friends of Piselli, and they cheered him on.

"*Bravo, Maestro!*" cried one.

"*Bravissimo! Che magnifico!*" another shouted.

I wanted to cheer also, but I felt too sorry for Piselli.

And poor Piselli, desperate now because he knew our project was forever doomed, played out the string. "What tragedy!" he shouted at the ancient dandy in the beige suede vest. The latter, eliciting compassion from me, was popping large turquoise pills into his mouth and sipping seltzer.

"What love!" sobbed the Maestro. "What crime!"

The Italian producer could bear it no longer. He leaped from his window seat and began clutching at Piselli's broad back, trying to detach him from the German lady.

"Buffoon! Pig! Fracturer of the reproductive organs!" the producer screamed—and really screamed. "Get off the floor! You have insulted our friend with your indecent actions!"

The game had ended. All dignity, Piselli rose—as magnificently as Botticelli's Venus from the bivalve.

"I am an artist," the director said stiffly. "I am not required to suffer the insults of financial persons." He picked up his floppy black Borsalino and nodded to Lucia Calmo (she, in turn, assembled the various scripts and outlines) and departed, amid cheers by the waiters. Lucia shot me a despairing look.

The ravished secretary assembled her limbs and got off the floor. I had to give her high marks; she was almost getting the best of Piselli when the producer broke it up. *Uberfraulein* that she was, her face remained frigid. No insane Italian would break down her Prussian impassivity.

There was a dull silence—the kind of theatrical letdown one experiences when Sir Laurence Olivier leaves the stage. The producer paced the floor, his hot eyes blazing. The elderly American kept munching pills. His shrewd old eyes blinked in the warm sunlight filtering through the high opened windows. Suddenly, the Italian producer turned to me.

"Gren," he pleaded, "you are an American, like Signor H—— here. Tell him what a great movie we have. Boxoffice. Sexy. Explain."

In my television days, I had been adept at what I call The Gambit of the Relevant Irrelevancy. This consists in redirecting the unfavorable turn of a discussion by introducing a factor only marginally related to the problem at hand, but possessing an intrinsic charm, or value, or glitter of its own. It worked marvels in meetings with disgruntled sponsors and unhappy high-priced talent. Yet I had the feeling, as I formulated strategy, that the tough old Beverly Hills type in the brocade chair was hardly the man to be suckered by my talker ploys. Nevertheless, I gave it a game try.

"It's really a great story," I lied. "Sex, crime, violence, teen-agers in blue jeans—all the things that have made movies better than ever. And lots of laughs. But what bothers me is the setting.

Why Iceland? Why that cold, bleak place that nobody cares about? Now it seems to me we might change the setting—and then we'd have a sure-fire hit. Instead of Iceland, we make it Naples. Instead of farmers, we make the family black-market operators. Tors becomes Torrio, the head of the cigarette syndicate. Sven is Savini. And so on. Everything drops into place— same story, same sex, same jokes. Only now it's a modern, sunny setting—Naples! And something that Maestro Piselli, and you, *Signore,* both understand well."

The Italian producer rubbed his nose. Clearly, I had proved a dud. "But the book takes place in Iceland," he said dully. "That's why I bought it. Naples is something else. I want to make a movie in Iceland."

We both awaited the moneyman's decision. In his high, thin voice, he finally said:

"I ain't interested. It's a costume picture."

Then, to my surprise, he turned to me, with a warm, sweet smile. "Young fellah," he said, "you know that tough old doctor you wrote about? How honest and courageous and moralistic he was? You coulda written that about me, kid. I'm the Last Angry Man, yessir. That was *my* life story."

It was time for me to go. We had come full circle. I saw in a filmy vision a convention of these hard old buccaneers, sweating in a luxurious steam bath somewhere in California, munching their dietetic foods, being massaged and fawned upon as part of their daily tribute, gliding about in air-conditioned Continentals —all convinced they were old Sam Abelman.

I thanked both men and made my way out to the dazzling sunlight on the Via Veneto. The Icelandic saga is still to be filmed—in Reykjavik or Naples.

Of all the people connected with our futile effort, I felt sorriest for Piselli. How could I not love a man, who, in broad daylight on the Piazza Navona, would plant his sturdy figure two inches to the rear of a fashionably dressed, lavender-haired, eminently attractive Italian *Signora* in her fifties, and announce to the world:

"Behold a woman filled with delights!"

My worries about the Maestro were soon allayed. Lucia Calmo, whom I would meet on the Veneto from time to time, told me he had been assigned to direct an adventure story in the Tyrol.

"Piselli is ecstatic," she said. "He is taking all those funny incidents we had in the Iceland story—the pants falling down, the fence breaking—and using them again. They are even better with a Tyrolean accent. The writer on the film is very devout, a Jesuitical type, and the Maestro scandalizes him."

I was glad that the *lire* that the Italian producer had paid out had not been wasted. The man had paid me scrupulously, on time, down to the last coin. However—the manner of payment deserves recounting, as a fitting conclusion to my exposure to the Italian cinema.

The MCA office in Rome called me in Rapallo one day to advise me that the check had arrived from the producer.

"Shall we deposit it for you in our account in Rome?" asked the MCA accountant, a young Italian lad.

"No," I said, "deduct your commission, and send me the balance here. I have a bank account in Rapallo, and could use some money."

Three days later, I trudged up the hill to Casa Stoppani, watching my children gathering snails—like hungry Sicilian peasants—and was met at the patio by Marie and an hysterical Filomena.

"Who sent you money?" Marie asked.

"Internal Revenue Service," I said. "They've probably realized what an awful thing they did to me two years ago."

"Not a check—cash. A big, fat wad of *lire*."

She held up a transparent plastic bag. Within I could see a thick roll of orange 10,000 lire notes. (Later that day I tried stuffing the roll down the mouth of a horse idling on the Lungomare; not only was it too big to choke him, it would not even fit in his maw.)

I took the bag from my wife. At the bottom were loose coins, some paper currency of smaller denomination. "Where did this come from?" I asked.

Marie turned to Filomena. The poor girl was trying to suppress hysteria. "A strange man, *Signor* Gren. He just came here and gave me all that money—for you." Her pretty features were working hard at diking tears. "So much money—I couldn't bear it. And he ran away. So I put it here—" (she indicated her bosom) "—to keep it safe until the *Signora* returned from the beach."

Marie took up the narration. "I came back and found her crying. I guess it's true. A man walked up, shoved a huge roll of 10,000 *lire* notes at her, plus some change and some small bills, and beat it. She says it wasn't even in an envelope—just a fistful of money. No message, no receipt. I put it in the plastic bag after Filomena extracted it from her brassiere."

"Oh, is anything wrong?" Filomena cried. "Has something bad happened?"

I could understand her terror. The amount of money was beyond her comprehension. And for such a sum to be tossed about in public, given to her without explanation, delivered by a mysterious stranger—all these smelled of evil work.

"Stop sniffling, Filomena," I said. "I am not an agent of the black market. I think this is the salary for the movie I worked on."

In the bedroom, we dumped the loot on a dresser and counted it. Down to the last lira, it was exactly what the producer owed me for my labor with Piselli—less agent's commission and government tax.

Somewhat annoyed at the business methods of MCA, I called the Rome office and spoke to its head, the bright young Italian lawyer. When I described the mode of delivery of my stipend—unpackaged, in cash, unreceipted, delivered by hand—he was mortified.

"I am terribly sorry," he said. "What did you tell our accountant? The boy has a very literal mind."

"I asked him to send me the money."

"Ah, but that is just what he did. He happened to have a day off, so he took the next train and personally went to Rapallo with the money."

"Why didn't he just mail me a check?"

"Ah, you did not ask for a check. You asked for the *money*."

That gave me pause. "But why no receipt? Or an envelope?"

The MCA man pondered a while. "The accountant wished to be economical. Besides, he felt it would be a sign of his greater honesty, and your trust in us, to deliver the cash loose."

"I appreciate his consideration, but he scared hell out of our maid. She carried it around in her brassiere all day."

I sent my regards to Piselli and Lucia and thanked him for the work.

So ended my brief association with the Italian film industry. It had begun at Piselli's villa, listening to the Maestro expound his theories of drama, and it had ended in Filomena's lovely bosom, inside a *Nailon* bra, with a C cup.

162

Often, I wonder what would have happened if the eager young accountant made the same error with a William Holden or a Marlon Brando. I envision a sun-drenched June morning on the Via Appia Antica, where the movie actors rent their villas. William Holden sits on his veranda, reading the financial pages of a Swiss newspaper. He looks up as an enormous truck suddenly backs into his driveway. The back of the truck opens, and three Italian laborers in blue overalls begin to shovel 10,000 lire notes on to the lawn.

The accountant then steps down from the cab of the truck and walks, hat in hand, up the old Roman stones on the walk, to the veranda. Holden rises to greet him—puzzled by the mountain of orange bills that has risen on his lawn.

"Your salary for the week, sir," the accountant says, "as you requested it."

CHAPTER twelve

Incoronata
and her children

Most little girls I have known seem to be interested in dolls, other little girls, and malicious gossip.

My daughter Nancy is no exception. During our Rapallo interlude, however, she developed one additional passion. She loves the European Common Market.

Where this passion for commerce comes, I cannot say. Her father had a bad time with Economics in college, and her mother has a worse time with check books.

I suspect her affection for the Common Market, all of its six members, began one day when Irving R. Levine, the National Broadcasting Company correspondent in Rome, and an old friend, visited us. Irving and I began to discuss the Common Market—the combined effort by France, West Germany, Italy, and the Benelux countries, to foster international trade among themselves.

Nancy listened most attentively. She was not yet seven.

"Daddy," she said after a while, "will the European Common Market make the poor people in Italy richer?"

"Well, we hope so," I said. "The idea is to lower the prices on the goods the different countries sell each other, and not to tax foreign goods so much. So if more people in the different countries can afford to buy more things, they can manufacture more and sell more and make more jobs."

"Oh Daddy, I love the European Common Market!" she cried. "Everybody should be for it! Is England for it?"

I tossed this to Levine, since he is still a working journalist. Having left this arena, I am required to know nothing at all.

"Not exactly," Irving said. "Oh, they're not against it, but they're not in it. They have their own group of countries—the Outer Seven."

"England should be in it," Nancy said, "if it will help the poor people in Italy." She frowned in the Mediterranean sunlight. "I know another way to help all the poor people."

"What's that, Nancy?" I asked.

She struggled to assemble words to fit her thoughts. "Well—if all the rich people in Italy, like Mr. Frezzolini, would give some of their money to all the poor people, like the chicken lady, then the poor people wouldn't be so poor anymore."

The chicken lady was a widow who lived high above us in the hills—beyond the hospital of the Mother Superior. She lived in an unheated, unelectrified stone house and supported three daughters by selling starved chickens. Nancy often played with her youngest girl.

Levine nodded his head. "Nancy should be invited to address the next joint session of the Italian parliament," he said. "Not that they'd listen to her—she makes too much sense."

This book is not intended as a compendium of insightful sayings by my children. Nor is it my intent to get involved in a long treatise on Italy's economic problems. But the essential truth of the Nancy Green Plan could not be denied. Perhaps a simple giving away of money was not the answer. But payment of taxes by the rich might be a good start. I love the country and its people—but I do not believe that poverty ennobles, or that there is anything charming about cities with 3,000 years of continuous civilization—and no running water.

Some weeks later, the impoverishment of the south of Italy— the *mezzogiorno*—was brought home to us in an intensely personal way. Marie had distant relatives in a remote village near Naples. On one of our forays away from the chi-chi of Rapallo, we visited them.

The trip south was memorable in many ways. Nancy, fortified with optimistic thoughts about the European Common Market (Irv Levine had promised to send her all available literature on the subject) tried to be brave about the grinding poverty that greeted us everywhere, particularly in the hills in back of Naples —our destination.

"You can tell when we get south," she said sadly. "Everything looks poorer."

"Well—at least they all have enough to eat," I said uneasily, doing the Italian government's dirty work for them.

166

"I can't wait for the European Common Market to start here," Nancy said. "Everything will be better."

Whenever we passed freight trains, or loaded trucks, or factories, she would point to them eagerly. "Look, Daddy! The European Common Market—it's making jobs for the Italians!"

My daughter's childish concern about the poor of Italy heartened me. She had reached these sentiments on her own—with no prodding from her do-gooding breast-beating liberal of a father. Not yet seven, she was prepared to have compassion for people living *in extremis,* to understand her common bond with the miserable peasants of the Campania. We grow old and we grow cynical; if we are newspaper editorialists we sneer at these sympathies as "do-gooding" or "breast-beating." But no one had brain-washed Nancy—her feelings were her own. I never heard her say that the poor people of Italy *deserved* what they got, because they were too lazy and stupid and rotten to help themselves.

The village where Marie's relatives lived was called Massadonia. It lay in the heart of the Campania, the depressed region which includes Naples, Salerno—and some of the worst poverty in Italy.

We drove first through the city of Avellino in a rainstorm, then took secondary roads into the hills, winding through rocky green heights, shorn of trees. It was a windy, oddly cold day. At the roadside, women swathed in black, almost Arab in their wrappings, rode by on stunted donkeys. Other women collected twigs in the stoney fields, even though it was a Sunday. In the sparse villages through which we drove, men were dressed in neat, dark clothing. There was little of the wild cheering and shouting we had come to expect when we drove in rural areas with the Citroen. These were solemn, leathery hill people. In the fifty-odd miles we traveled from Naples to Massadonia, we did not pass more than four automobiles. The villages we raced through seemed devoid of shops—perhaps a single shabby bar, one tiny grocery.

By now, Nancy was dismally silent. She knew that her mother's grandma—her own great grandmother—had lived here. Widowed, she had borrowed some money and come to America with three small children. My daughter's troubled silence moved me. I suspect we perpetually underestimate the depths of feeling in our children. Is it because as we age, we lose our own capacity to feel for others—like the congressmen and editorialists who sneer at do-gooders?

We approached Massadonia on a rutted, twisting road. Apparently it had once been blacktopped. But now its surface was an ugly admixture of crumbled tarmac, yellow dirt and native gray stone. As we climbed, the town loomed above us—graybrown, graceless, morosely advertising its misery, its defeat. Here was no ancient charm, no relic of a glorious past. Massadonia was simply poor, arid and unhappy.

As I turned a corner and entered the town proper, I was halted by a middle-aged man with a luxurious black mustache. He was in shirt-sleeves, but wore a policeman's cap. Another Lentini, obviously.

"Permit me," he said. "I am the Chief of Police. It is my function to show visiting Americans to the homes of their relatives."

I asked him where we could find a woman named Incoronata Melfi. He saluted me, ducked into his building, and returned in a few minutes, buttoning on his tunic.

"My files are very complete. I have located her," he said. The usual crowd had gathered around the car, cautiously admiring the manner in which it wheezed up and down. I noticed that the streets, while narrow, ugly and ancient, were spotlessly clean.

"Melfi Incoronata," the chief said, "lives nearby. I make sure to escort visitors personally."

We rode between rows of pitted, crumbling two story houses. There was nothing colorful or quaint about Massadonia.

The chief chattered on: *Hi Joe, Okay. Choon Gum.* He was rather like Lentini, at that. He even seconded Lentini's opinion that Brooklyn was the most beautiful place in the world. Like Lentini, he knew because he had cousins there.

There was not a single automobile in Massadonia—not even a motor scooter! We were at rock bottom in the Italian economic scale.

In the drab village square, a crowd of young men in dark suits hooted at us—not menacingly, or with jealousy—but with that faintly mocking friendliness with which all Americans are greeted. I suspect they know they can get away with it with rich Americans, whom, it is assumed, are descendants of their own poor neighbors.

There was a fountain in the piazza—the eternal fountain. It was old, cracked, dirty—and a silent queue of about a dozen people were lined up for water. It was not quite as beautiful as the Trevi or the Fiume in Piazza Navona, but it had a certain powerful significance. No one threw coins in Massadonia's fountain.

"Oh, are we far south," Nancy said. "This is the poorest we've seen yet."

We turned up a cobbled street and stopped at an old stone house. The windows and the door had been painted a bright blue.

169

"This is the house of Melfi," the policeman said. I tipped him, and he left—reminding me to recommend him to all visiting *Americani*.

Now I must preface what I have to say with a personal note. Persons who have read my novels must be aware that I am hardly a sentimentalist where the poor are concerned. I do not believe that poverty breeds virtue in people, or that the lower layers of human society are noted for their good behavior. Quite the contrary: not having enough to eat, living in subhuman habitation, suffering the degradation of unemployment, usually works the other way with people. Crime, bad manners, a corrosion of whatever is sensitive and sensible in men, is the expectable result. What I have to say now about the Melfi household, then, is hardly the report of a hopeless romantic.

We knocked at the blue door. A woman opened it. She appeared to be in her mid-fifties—heavily built, muscular, short, with a round, red face in which the features were blunted and roughened by wind and sun. Yet it was far from a dull face. Her eyes were black and vivacious. She wore mourning black—the mourning that never ends. In the south, women wear black for a year to mark the death of any remotely related person. Since families are large, there are usually enough deaths to keep the women in black perpetually. (G. Green, economic determinist wonders if there is not a pragmatic basis to this. Black doesn't show dirt.)

"*Americani? Parenti?*" she asked. "Relatives?"

Marie held her arms out. "I'm Maria Anna, the daughter of your second cousin Lucia in America. Do you remember, Incoronata—she came to see you two years ago?"

The woman wailed, wept, hugged Marie and dragged us into the house. Marie introduced me, then introduced Nancy—"An-

170

nunziatina"—the name her grandmother called our daughter by.

There followed three or four minutes of hugs, tears, shouts, prayers, invocations of the Virgin, Saint Joseph, and lesser holy persons. A select group of neighbors gathered on the steps to join in the applause. Incoronata shooed them away and made us welcome.

The house consisted of two sagging rooms, and a small alcove for cooking. In the latter was an ancient, blackened wood burning stove. A single electric light bulb dangled in the combined living-dining room. The bedroom was at the rear. The floors were stone. In the main room was one scarred, canted table, several haphazard chairs, and a sloping, glassless closet that held a half dozen dishes.

"My husband is not here today," she apologized. "He works, even Sunday. He is a guard in the fields."

Incoronata explained that both she and her husband worked for a big *padrone* whom no one ever saw. He lived in Rome and had overseers run the farming. Since her husband was a war veteran, wounded in Africa, he had the privilege of working Sunday for extra money as an armed guard. Theft of crops was frequent.

"Oh, we are so poor," she said—not seeking sympathy, merely setting the record straight. "I am ashamed of this house and the terrible old things we have. But what can we do? There are no jobs in Massadonia—only the fields."

As she spoke of their poverty, she did not whine. The subject of her discourse was depressing—her style was not. I had the feeling that if Incoronata's income could be doubled, she would have made the ascent into the middle class with no effort. There

171

was no inherent weakness in her; only the weakness inspired by a feudal, blundering society.

"Yes, everyone goes away from here," she said to Marie. As she spoke she gestured vigorously with her hard, red hands. "I had three brothers. Two went to Turin to work in the factories. The oldest went to Australia. He left his wife and two kids, but he stopped writing, stopped sending money. My husband and I help her out. I had three sisters, God bless them. Two are dead. The third moved, with her husband to Milan, but he only works part of the time. The Milanese don't like us southerners. They call us monkeys, Arabs, Negroes. But believe me, we'd move also—if we knew where to go. Well, it could be worse. Our *padrone,* whoever he is, isn't as bad as some. He lets us keep our own chickens and a piece of land to grow vegetables. So we all eat enough—but food isn't everything."

She threw up her hands—despairing of her recital, suddenly aware that she was failing at trying to make the best of things.

"Ah, we should have moved away with the others. There used to be 15,000 people in Massadonia. Now—7,000. Who wants to stay where there's no work? Oh, your Grandma was the smartest—she went to America. And my *nonna* should have done the same. They were the same age then—neighbors."

I was puzzled for a moment. Marie's grandmother and Incoronatas were of the same generation—first cousins. Yet Incoronata, for all her high spirits and vigor, appeared to be in her early fifties, perhaps fifteen years older than Marie.

"How old are you, Incoronata?" I asked.

The ruddy, round face beamed—the black eyes snapped. "Me? I'm a kid—*bambina*. I'm 38."

She was a young woman. Wind, sun, poverty, and that anxiety which we stupidly assume is the burden only of the secure and

172

sophisticated, had beaten a dozen more years into her face. Why must we always be so convinced that the poor of the world are too ignorant to know that they're poor, too lazy to want anything better, and sufficiently generous to go on forgiving the rich forever?

Yet there was a miracle in Incoronata. There was no real surrender in her voice. Her capacities for life, for love had not been buried in that hard ground of the Campania. Endlessly, she would complain about their miserable lot, but, please note, the complaints were made in a loud, strong voice—not a coward's whine—and she almost seemed to be petitioning someone, anyone—*give us a chance!* I must repeat again that these are cold, objective observations on my part. I am congenitally opposed to assuming virtue in the poor.

Incoronata's three children entered. A neighbor, an old lady in a black shawl, distantly related, ushered them in—and promptly smothered me in kisses. The children marched in solemnly, with a subdued excitement. There was a girl of 15, stocky and dark like her mother, and two smaller children—a boy, Mario, who was 8, and a girl Francesca, who was 6. The two younger children were fair, with ash-blond hair and gray eyes. Incoronata explained that her husband was *biondo*. The three lined up to be introduced to us, shaking hands and kissing us. They grinned at Nancy, patted her hair, touched her dress.

"These are my *tesori*—my treasures," Incoronata said. "Angelina is the oldest, and she still goes to school, which is hard for us to do, but I will keep her in school until we have no more money. The nuns say she is very intelligent."

The children were neatly dressed, their clothes old, but clean. There were patches on Mario's trousers and Francesca's sweater was faded. Their manners—I am embarrassed to report they were *perfect*, better than the usual behavior of our own hoodlums.

We opened a valise to give them some clothing we had brought from Rapallo—Marie's mother had told us the ages of the children—and they laughed and teased one another, trying on shirts, shoes, sweaters. We looked on sadly—rich Americans who had always had enough clothing, enough food, promise of work. Poor Nancy was staring at them—confounded.

Incoronata chased the older girl out of the house to the local bar to buy a pot of coffee—a luxury. We were guests and merited the delicacy. Then, she herself hurried out the back of the house and returned with a box of still-warm eggs and two brown wicker baskets.

"Fresh stuff!" she shouted. "From the country—better than the store!" She up-ended the baskets, and two white cheeses dropped out. "Taste!" she cried—hacking off a slice for me. It was delicious—a variety of hard ricotta, creamy, faintly musty.

I objected to her generosity. I refused to take the food. She would not listen. Already, she was wrapping each egg in newspaper, deftly fitting them into the empty valise. I tried to explain we had a long trip home, and the eggs might not keep.

"No, no! This fresh food is good for the *bambini!* See how healthy my kids are—even though we're poor!"

I watched her as she wrapped the eggs and the cheese. Her hands were scarlet and calloused. Her clothes, I now noticed, were terribly shabby. A huge rusted safety pin held the black shawl together over her bosom. And then I looked at her children —delighting in the new clothes. They were clean, polite, intelligent—anything but the products of degradation and meanness. Suddenly I had a madman's vision—Incoronata and her neighbors in Massadonia as guests of honor at one of Checkovich's

174

friend's villas in Portofino: peasant honored by parasite. Was it not fitting that the moneyed nitwits and non-tax-paying boobs who ran the place occasionally pay tribute to the people who let them do it?

"Oh, you'll come visit again!" Incoronata shouted. "You'll write to me before, so I can prepare a country dinner for you— *una cena rustica!* I can do no less for Maria, the daughter of my cousin Lucia in America!"

At last eggs and cheese were secured in the valise. I took Incoronata into the back room and gave her some money. She hugged me and began to sniffle. There were no coy protests about not needing the money, no false shame, no effort to discourage me. She damned well needed the money, and she was grateful.

It was time to go. Outside, I could hear Nancy squeaking in Italian—she was playing tag with her fourth (or fifth) cousins. Marie was talking to the older girl—who was unhappy because there were not enough young men in Massadonia. They all went north or to Australia.

"We must leave now," I said. "We have far to travel."

Incoronata protested. "No—I will make the *cena rustica* to-night. Angelina—go get your father from the fields! Mario—run to Assunta's house and see if she will lend us some pasta! We will have guests tonight!"

We assured her that her generosity was appreciated—the eggs and cheese were ample. There were more kisses and hugs, a few tears. The old lady from next door, no kin to any of us, did most of the weeping. I don't think she was quite certain who we were, or why we were there—but she was not going to pass up a chance for a harmless emotional workout.

The children lined up again to say their goodbyes.

"Arrivederci, cugina Annunziatina," they said to Nancy.

Embarrassed, all Nancy could say was: *"Ciaou."*

We drove off—to a round of applause for the Citroen. Incoronata, a stubby black figure, ran a few steps after us calling:

"Kiss your Mama and Papa for me! And you will all come back soon to eat with us!"

In a few minutes we were speeding down the fragmented old road, past the police station, where the Chief waved at us, past an ancient seminary, where a troop of black-robed novitiates paraded by solemnly, on to the arid plateau that led back to Avellino and Naples.

Marie was crying.

"It's a crime," she said. "It's a crime against the human race. So poor, so *poor*. And what's worse—nothing to look forward to. No place to go. No jobs. No future. No chance to improve. Nothing better for their children—ever. And did you see those kids? Did you ever see better kids?"

I agreed; we had been stunned by the children—not just Incoronata's, but all the children of Massadonia. They were—how shall I put it? They were children with *quality*. As impoverished as were their lives, as marginal their daily existence, they were children with the marks of breeding, good manners, intelligence. They were no dirt-smeared, runny-nose, mumbling collection of hill-dwellers. They were heirs to an old, viable civilization.

"Our kids should have such good manners," I said—with an arch glance at Nancy, huddled in the back seat. "But I'll excuse ours. They don't have 3,000 years of continuous civilization in back of them."

"Why doesn't somebody do something?" Marie cried. "Jobs, factories, anything! Every time I pass a textile mill or a road

176

building project from now on, I'll stand up and cheer. I've got nothing against the museums and the churches, I like them also. But that can be your department. Me, I'll go visit the cement works."

"Honey, it's a poor country. Overpopulated. Not enough resources—no coal, no iron, no oil. Just people."

"But that's it!" Marie said. "People! It's the best resource they have—the people. But the idiots who run the place haven't realized it yet. Look at Incoronata and those kids—those are the resources. Don't tell me they're lazy and stupid and dishonest. Who isn't—if he doesn't get half a chance? Why, they've got more strength and vigor and ambition and brains than all those waxworks in Portofino, together!"

We had learned something—and another myth had died. The poor of Massadonia—and later we found the same to be true of the people of Calabria and Sicily—are, for the most part, people of enormous potential. They cannot be fairly compared to the slum poor of America—our depressed urban minorities, or the impoverished rural whites of the south. Why do I say this? Because the Italian poor have the benefit of a long, continuous tradition. They are no degraded horde—like the street sleepers of India, or the howling mobs of Cairo. They possess the powerful remnants of high civilization—family tradition, humor, a willingness to learn and to work. Forget all the cliches about the south. Just remember that its people are waiting for a chance—anything to improve their lot—jobs, schools, a jot of dignity. I have spoken to several American businessmen who have started factories in the Naples area. All were unanimous in praising the talents of the Italian workmen.

Of course there are scattered pockets of violence and crime—parts of Naples, western Sicily. But for the most part, again in contradiction of the mythology, they are a remarkably law abiding people. Centuries of domination by foreigners, absentee landlords, and armed overseers have imbued them with a wariness of lawbreaking. One is a lot safer strolling through the streets of Palermo, alone, at midnight, than one is in Central Park—in broad daylight.

"Some day it will happen," I said. "It has to happen. A couple of rich, influential Italians will say—let's do it—and it will start to change."

"From your mouth and in God's ear," said Marie—paraphrasing an old Hebrew adage. "I keep thinking of all those dummies in Portofino and the Via Veneto. Will they let it happen?"

"They'd better."

It was raining now, a thin hesitant rain, as sapped of strength as the old earth, the tired fields that surrounded us. The land had lost its vigor, but the people had not. That was the miracle of Italy—the undying strength of the poor. Like Incoronata and her bright, prideful children, they sit, and wait, and wait—for opportunities that never seem to come. But they are patient, with limits. The Communist vote does *not* get smaller.

We rode in silence past the hovels of farm laborers, the sad flaking villages, the treeless, rocky fields. Suddenly Nancy's voice piped up—soft, pensive, without its usual cutting edge.

"Daddy," she said, "why didn't you tell our cousins about the European Common Market? I bet the Common Market will help them a whole lot."

"That's right, honey, I should have," I said. "We will next time."

I would be the last man in the world to discourage a child's hopes, or scoff at economic planning.

178

CHAPTER thirteen

the good-natured
American

Will someone please step forward and say a few kind words for the American tourist?

Nobody? None of you professional Europe-lovers? Very well, I will. I was going to anyway.

Among the persistent myths of our time is the one that holds that the American overseas traveler is a boor, a loudmouth, a materially-minded intruder, who rudely tosses dollars around Europe, while making sneering comments about the paintings, the plumbing, and the local politics. This lout turns up every-

179

where, I am told. He is a disgrace to the United States, a betrayer of our foreign policy, and—you know the rest of the argument. I hear it every time I go to a Fairfield County cocktail party.

Lies, all lies. During the four months we were in Rapallo, and the ensuing fourteen months in Rome, we travelled considerably. We observed many, many Americans. We also saw Germans, English, French, Scandinavians, Latin Americans and Orientals. Of all members of the *genus tourismus,* your American is the politest, the most considerate, the most cheerful, and the most generous. Please let us not forget this last attribute—goodness knows no European ever forgets it.

Let me start with a specific example, then go on to the general. We were on a guided tour of Versailles. It was an American Express affair, but we were in the harsh hands of the French— sixty sweating Americans, laden with cameras, guidebooks and goodwill. Enough has been written about the rudeness of our French allies, so I feel somewhat guilty adding my own tithe. But how could I ever forget our tall, lissome lady cicerone, whom I asked in rather good French, whether there were special tours of the Louvre? She curled a luscious lip at me. "There are," she answered, in English poorer than my French, "but they are only in French, and one must understand French to appreciate fully the works of art."

She had told me one untruth and one insult. As I learned the next day, there are English-language tours of the Louvre every hour—so she was at best, misinformed. At worst, she was fibbing, just to annoy me. And why the gratuitous insult? My French is reasonably good—surely good enough to understand a Parisian guide. She had heard me speak French. Why the nasty comment that one had to understand it to appreciate the works of art? Are paintings better when described in French?

So there we were, at the mercy of this Venus in a blue uniform and a Bardot hairdo. There were, as I said, threescore of us, happy people from Brooklyn, Des Moines and Medford, Oregon, crammed into a devilishly hot bus, off to Versailles. It was one of those ingeniously designed buses in which extra seats unfold into the aisle, thus blocking movement or breathing.

While we were still in Paris, the lady guide, who had already sandbagged me and my artistic pretensions, went to work on two old ladies from Niles, Michigan. (I adore elderly American ladies seeing Europe on their own. They are forever brave, good-natured, energetic. I suspect most of them are schoolteachers, and I have always been a sucker for schoolteachers.) In any event, Bardot accused them of having the wrong tickets for the Versailles tour. They explained tearfully that the concierge at their hotel had gotten them a package deal—four tours, of which they had made three already. None of the *other* guides had told them they were wrong.

But the guide was adamant. She all but threatened to throw them off the bus. At length the mystery was solved—the concierge had scrawled the wrong date on the tickets. The elderly American ladies were right, and she was wrong. But she did not apologize for her nastiness.

The vignette haunts me with bothersome clarity: the sexy young woman, bright with Gallic style, insulting those poor old souls as if they had just voted to end the Economic Aid Program. And my countrywomen! Clumsily garbed they were, in cottons, gum-soled shoes and floppy straw hats—their faces troubled, their voices shaking. I had the uneasy sensation that they were being chastised simply for being Americans. The guide envisioned herself as *Europa* (the bus her white bull?) having her revenge on these *arrivistes* from the New World.

181

I do not intend this essay as an intemperate attack on the French, or on Europeans in general. But is it not possible that we Americans, notably our so-called elite, have gone a little haywire in the way in which we criticize our fellow citizens when they are exposed to Europe? Why is it that *anything* an American does overseas at once becomes the subject for sneer and contempt by our professional Europe-lovers? (I myself am a Europe-liker.)

What is so dreadful about wearing loose, comfortable, yes, loud clothing—nylon shirts and dacron dresses? Is there an inherent sin in gum-soled shoes? Are we to be forever damned because we trudge about churches and museums laden with Rolleiflexes and Bolexes and exposure meters? Why is an American smoking a cigar an oaf, while a Tuscan farmer puffing a stogie, or a Swiss businessman chewing a Rossli 7, are regarded as quaint and natural?

Must we forever assume that the European is more cultured, better-mannered, more gracious, less materialistic? Rudeness knows no boundaries, and I would suggest that your average Roman motorist ranks high on the scale of international impoliteness. Ah, but he is not alone. The average German traveler, I have found, is much louder and more boorish than the average American. He stomps about in hiking shoes and lederhosen, laughing uproariously as he revisits scenes of past Wehrmacht glory. And the French get good marks also. Try arguing with a Paris concierge over a bill of twelve dollars for pressing—not dry cleaning, just pressing—four dresses. And this at a third class hotel! (Maybe I should go easy on the French. I suspect these unpleasantries are typical more of Paris, and of tourist Paris. In the provinces, there is usually a bit more friendliness.)

As for materialism, no nation has a monopoly on it. We are always singled out because we have so much more. But just give the European a chance. An Italian loves his car more than his wife—more than his mistress. He washes it with an ardor that I have never seen equalled in Nassau County. And he knows less about the frescoes in the church down the block than he does about the price of a carburetor.

To get back to that tour of Versailles. (Incidentally, it cured us forever of taking these packaged visits. From then on, we struggled with our own guide books—much more fun—except in vast places like Pompeii or Herculaneum, where we splurged on a private guide. Good investments.) It was the end of May, but Paris was already swarming with visitors. When we got to the Palace, we were swiftly herded through the rooms by our surly lady, like so many steers headed for slaughter.

Versailles was packed to the limit. The only crush of bodies to equal it that I can recall, was at a Memorial Day double-header at Yankee Stadium in the thirties, when the departing crowd came to a dead halt on the ramps for twenty minutes. Later, a fan tried to sue the New York Yankees for false imprisonment.

We shuffled through the ornate, gilded, draped rooms, gawking, barely hearing the guide's bored lecture—and finally came to a complete stop. For fifteen minutes we were stuck, eyes glassy, legs trembling, amid the Bourbon splendours. Versailles simply could hold no more of us. We were immobilized. As we inched our way from chamber to chamber, dazzled by the gaudy fixtures of bad kings, it was the lady guide who became increasingly ill-tempered. More and more, her sullen lectures were laced with sarcastic comments—which we Americans were either too polite or too naive to appreciate.

"Zis room," she said, "is ze gold room. Eet is where ze King would grant audiences, if you are aware of what such things are."

After a half-dozen of these darts, I realized that the beauty had consciously cast herself in the role of cultured, lovely Europe, uncomfortable in the swarm of American clods. This attitude is not limited to French guides. I have experienced it, to a lesser extent elsewhere. In Italy, for all the friendliness of the guides, one is forever being reminded of the way we bombed their art treasures—notably Monte Cassino.

"Ah, you insisted on bombing the Germans," a gracious Contessa working as a guide told me, "and you ruined our precious Abby." She did not react favorably when I suggested that if her countrymen had fought the Germans a little more vigorously, Monte Cassino might have been spared our explosives. Come to think of it, we paid to rebuild it, didn't we?

In Madrid, a guide haughtily accused a party of Americans of a lack of sympathy for General Franco; in London, one of those long-wavy-haired crypto-poets, with a false upper class accent, informed a party of midwesterners, with a snide giggle: "I s'pose we're quits now! We've given the wehld Shakespeare, and you've given the wehld Coca-Cola!"

(In passing, I have thought of something nice to say about Switzerland. It is a small country, with no art, indifferent architecture and well-planned cities. It's all scenery and chocolate, neither of which require guided tours.)

And what of my fellow-Americans from Boise, Glens Falls and New Bern, North Carolina?

Proud am I to report that through this fog of snidery, these pepperings of impertinence, these repeated reminders of our ignorance, callousness and materialism, they took it bravely and with good humor. In Versailles, where we stood impacted in room after vulgar room, their friendly, patient nasalized voices rose around me.

"Hey, Verne, watch your Kodak, you're gettin' awful personal."

"Ain't my fault, Lamar. Somebody just shoved me. Hey, lady, we haven't even been introduced."

"Well, it don't take much to make friends in a mob like this."

"Didn't those old boys spend dough on themselves? Imagine all the fertilizer you could buy for what it cost to paint those walls gold?"

"Sssh, Baxley, the guide is talkin' again."

"Heck, she isn't gonna do anything but pass a few more remarks. She's a regular Frenchie Herb Shriner, that one."

Examine these comments. Boorish? Cruel? Evidence that we are a decadent and vulgar people? I hardly think so. Rather I find a good-natured tolerance in my countrymen. I kept finding it all over Europe. A mythic figure keeps cropping up in tourist lore—the florid, loud-mouthed American on the airplane who makes a pass at the BOAC hostess, upsets the champagne and insults Churchill—but I confess I never met him. Of course, there are some nasty American tourists. But I submit, we are hypersensitive about them, and use them as the paradigm—instead of the battalions of American pilgrims who spend liberally, behave properly and show both a genuine interest in and tolerance for the Old World.

Here, I am forced to add an aside about Versailles—one prompted by my fellow-tourist's comment in terms of fertilizer. After all, what *is* so beautiful about Versailles? In both execution and in import, I find it dubious. If you will, I find it a tower of vulgarity, a tribute to a vain, self-indulged, irresponsible and ultimately self-destructive mode of life. Since I am a writer, and consequently more of a public hypocrite than the touring farmers from Ames, Iowa, and the hardware merchants from Shamokin,

185

Pennsylvania, I rarely verbalized my misgivings about the abundance of ornate monuments to bad kings and questionable clerics.

It is essential here that I establish my credentials as a fellow who likes Art. What I have just said about many of Europe's treasures is not to be taken as generalized scorn for every museum and cathedral. But there are treasures and treasures. There is, I believe, a vast gulf between the pomposity, the corrupt glitter of a Versailles, and the colorful purity of a Pinturicchio or a Beato Angelico. One is not required to ooh and ah over everything in Europe, even though the guides and the guide books extol them. In the Ducal Palace in Venice, one of the purported masterpieces is Tintoretto's *Paradise*, the world's largest oil painting on canvas—22 x 7 metres. If this is Paradise, Heaven can wait. This enormous painting is surely the most reassuring evidence extant for a non-believer. It is guaranteed to warm any atheist's heart. What a mad confusion of whirling, gnarled, reaching, writhing bodies—all bathed in a ghastly ultra-violet light! It is not only bad theology, it is bad painting. Odd, that the books never warn us about all the dreadful stuff turned out during the Renaissance.

Go to the Doria Palace in Rome, and you will see what I mean. For the half dozen absolute masterpieces there—including Velasquez' portrait of Innocent X—you will be forced to struggle through yards of plodding junk, the 16th and 17th century equivalents of the Washington Square Outdoor Exhibit.

But struggle through much of this my beloved American tourist does. He sees the good and the bad, and rarely does he complain, or play the role of unkind critic. He accepts Europe with a warm smile, and a lively sense of humor. He does not keep reminding them that we are saving them from Com-

186

munism, or won their wars. Far from it. More often it is the European who has complaints to register about us—the way our planes destroyed their villages, the way our soldiers corrupted their women. Good God—didn't the Germans *ever* drop a bomb?

These reflections on Americans in Europe, what is expected of them, and how they actually do behave, brings me to the matter of the present-day U.S. serviceman abroad. During the last war (the one before Korea) I spent two years in Europe as an enlisted man—England, France, Germany. My recollections have become rather hazed, now that my Eisenhower jacket fits my son Teddy better than it does me, and the Ordnance bomb on the lapel is rusting. But I am reasonably certain that American troops set some kind of record overseas for alcoholism, skirt-chasing, intemperate language and general rough behavior. You know the old English gag: Name three things wrong with the GI's. Answer: *Overpaid, Oversexed and Over Here.*

All this, I can report on the basis of close observations in Rapallo, has changed.

Our American boys in foreign lands are a collection of Billy Grahams.

We had evidence in Rapallo. The United States Navy put into port for four days. It was the first week of July—a combined Independence Day Holiday and an observance of the Festa of the Virgin of Mont'Allegre, Rapallo's patroness. There were two supply ships in harbor, and in a few hours the town swarmed with our white-jacketed lads. Our children were fascinated; Marie and I were genuinely glad to see them. In my case, certain lush memories of mad weekend passes in the English Midlands came back to me. I would be pleased to see a new generation of fighting men carrying on the hell-raising traditions. Poignantly, I longed for my old Sergeant's uniform—the good conduct medal, the hash mark, the four overseas bars.

"Look out now, baby," I told Marie. "This joint will never recover after our sailors work it over."

"You look like you're ready to join in the boozing."

"Yeah!" I sighed. "Wouldn't I love to! It'll be just as much fun to watch. Poor old Rapallo and Portofino—they'll never recover."

Nostalgically, I watched the young gobs descend on our particular beach club, the Lido.

Naturally, our kind of club drew only the enlisted personnel. The officers appeared to have vanished. Here is a mystery I would like cleared up—possibly by someone in the Pentagon. Where do the officers go? Why is it that they vanish, disappear, evanesce, whenever a naval vessel has leave, or a division gets time off? There are always lots of enlisted men—hordes of seamen and corporals and sergeants. But where are the officers? Oh Captain, my Captain! Are they all agents of the CIA, melting into civilian obscurity to make deals with Portuguese couriers and counter-agents? Are they mingling among us, in mufti, performing secret errands for Alan Welsh Dulles? Or are they ferried ashore in the dead of night to private palaces of delights, forbidden to the lower ranks? During the four days our Navy, which I help support, was in Rapallo, I saw only one officer. He was a pale ensign, who evidently had not gotten word, or for personal reasons, was not included in the secret plans of the gold stripe set. All right there, Pentagon, let's have it—where are the officers?

If there was a lack of commanders and lt's. (jg) there was surely no dearth of enlisted men in Rapallo. They settled on the Lido like clouds of white doves—neat, eager, polite boys, trying desperately to make friends with the Italian *borghese*. I should

188

have warned them not to waste their time. The upper class Italian speaks to no one except blood relatives, and perhaps one or two associates on his own level. All others he avoids—those who rank him socially won't give him the time of day, and those below him are worthy only of contempt. Foreigners are to be guarded against at all times—they are unpredictable.

Much has been written and mumbled about the magical effect that the American sailor in his bell-bottoms has on foreign girls. It is nonsense, all nonsense. At least it is nonsense along the Riviera in peacetime. The Italian ladies at our Lido, single or married, that entrancing brigade of high-stepping half-mooners, waggling and wobbling by in bikinis and simpers, were about as approachable as porcupines. Our jack tars tried again and again —and were rewarded with blank stares, sneers and a final turn of butt and departing wobble.

In fairness, I must report that the sailors did not try terribly hard. There were no pinches, pats, prods or passes. There were halting attempts at Italian conversation—that got nowhere. Despondent, our gentle young men returned to the warm Swiss beer which the proprietor of the bar had judiciously stocked in anticipation of the fleet. Equally judiciously, he had found it provident to double the price. It was dreadful beer.

By late morning, the height of the beach day (at 1:00 PM, as I have recounted elsewhere, the Great Curve of Life begins its ascent to the pasta) there were several hundred sailors on the Lido. About half were in swimsuits, the others in their whites. Being a naive unrepentant humanist, I was happy to see many Negroes, Filipinos and Orientals mingling freely with the white lads. Our armed forces, I am pleased to note, so long considered hotbeds of reaction, have been way ahead of the rest of us in blunting the harsh edges of racism.

189

The boys appeared to be enjoying themselves, but it wasn't quite what I had expected of them. To begin with, the Italians and the other foreigners on the Lido avoided them as if they were disease carriers. There was no overt repugnance, no nasty comments, nothing resembling a spat. They simply ignored our boys. The Americans did not exist. Particularly, they did not exist for the ladies—those gay, chi-chi, mad girls Fodor had told me about in his otherwise admirable guide book.

Why had it been so different the last time I was with enlisted men? Memories of London under the blitz, Paris liberated, Bremen occupied came back to me—girls so eager to welcome the conqueror. I had a vision of a mile long parade of couples— he in khaki or blue, raincoat over arm, pockets a-bulge with chocolate and cigarettes and soap, she in faded woolen coat and cotton stockings, promenading in international amity. Sweethearts on parade. All that, I am afraid, has vanished.

Partly, I suppose the coldness of the European woman toward our uniformed male, is the result of the vitiating effects of peace and prosperity. We liberated Europe from the Germans, and the Europeans were grateful. We are supposedly liberating Europe from the Russians now, but as far as I know, the Russians have never occupied Italy. Of course, a few Russians were there for the Treaty of Rapallo, that disturbing rapprochement between the Soviet Union and the Weimar Republic, which still haunts the chancellories of Europe.

(This is as good a time as any for my personal report on the Treaty of Rapallo, signed in 1922. Feeling rather like Walter Lippman and one Alsop, I sought out an informant, who had been in Rapallo when the Germans and Russians assembled for the parley and the eventual pact. "Tell me all you remember about the conference," I asked the elderly gentleman, who was a pharmacist by trade. "Oh, I recall it very well," he said. "Yes, yes," I pursued, "did you have occasion to meet the delegates, to sound them out on the future of Russo-German relations?" He pondered. "Many times I saw them," the pharmacist said. "They all came to my pharmacy to shop. Rathenau bought aspirin and razor blades. Oil of cloves, I think. Chicherin was in quite often. He purchased throat lozenges. But Trotsky! He was the most fascinating, that terrible Bolshevik!" I was panting. "Tell me, tell me about Trotsky!" I cried. The pharmacist ruminated. "Trotsky bought laxatives. Cascara. Rhubarb and Soda. Psyllium Seeds. Trotsky was constipated.")

But this was 1959 and there were no eager women to accept kisses and coffee, no kids to reach out grubby hands for chocolate and chewing gum. So our nice young sailors sipped beer, swam, joked, played chess, and took long rides in horse-drawn carriages.

It saddened me. "Gosh, what a shame," I said to Marie. "Look at the way the vigor, the virility of our armed forces have deteriorated. When I was an enlisted man—"

"I know, I know. You and the 827th Ordnance Base Depot Company started a whiskey riot in Leamington Spa one night. Hero. You are old, fat, bald, and your GI pants don't fit you."

"But it's all wrong—the way these kids are behaving themselves. Mythology says that the American enlisted man is loud, boorish, sex-mad, drunk and insulting. He pinches the mayor's daughter and throws Baby Ruths at starving children who are allergic to nuts and chocolate."

Angrily, I turned to Nancy. "Hey you," I commanded, "run over to those sailors and make believe you're an urchin. Beg for lire. Demand chocolate—in Italian. Rub dirt on your nose. Make them feel at home."

Ever ready for adventure, Nancy, browner than any Italian

kid (remember, they're raised under glass) scampered over to the American encampment.

"Was that a good idea?" Marie asked. "My father always warned me to stay away from sailors."

"Yes, and look at you." July was a bad month all around. You will recall it was the time we surrendered Mavis and the comfort of Villa Frezzolini for the joys of the What-A-Stink River; the time of Lentini and Legs and the TV set burning on the top floor. We did not know it then, but August would be worse— Nardulli and his gang of *zoccoli*-wearers were yet to come.

After a while, I strolled over to see how Nancy was doing and whether my tax dollar was being put to good use. She had retrogressed to slangy English, was wearing a Chief Petty Officer's white cap and was sipping *aranciata*.

A chubby lad with an Ohio accent thrust a bottle of Coke at me. "Golly, you must be Mr. Green the writer," he said. "I sure liked your book. Reminded me of my grampa. He was a druggist just like that ole Doctor."

Others soon crowded around me. They were innocent, all innocent. As nice a crowd of high school cheer leaders as I have ever seen. The average age was twenty-one. The median accent was midwestern. The manners were good, the sense of humor unstrained, pleasant. Ah, my Americans, what nonsense is written about you!

"It sure is nice to let Nancy visit," a slender boy said, in pure, clear Californese. "Reminds me of my little sister back home in Santa Monica."

I cleared my throat. "I guess you fellows are just resting up— getting ready to paint the town red tonight, hey?"

Their faces grew solemn. The chess game stopped. A tall Texan walked up to me. "Why, lord-a-mighty no, Mr. Green.

We're under strict orders to behave ourselves. We have the responsibility of bein' goodwill ambassadors."

At first I thought he was needling me. But it was evident that he was sincere. Others supported his sentiment—a Warner Brothers platoon. There was a wise-cracking Brooklyn Italian, a hill boy from Marietta, Georgia, a wheat farmer's son from Kansas, a copper miner from Utah.

"Ah, come on fellows," I laughed. "Look—you don't have to kid me. I was an enlisted man myself once. I know what it's like. There was one night in Henly-in-Arden, that's this little town in Warwickshire, when our outfit had to fight it out with the Royal Signal Corps for the rights to a dance hall, and me and two guys from Alabama stole a fork-lift truck and—"

Silence greeted my War Memoirs; a deep, solemn silence.

"Shucks, Mr. Green," the tall Texan said, after a while. "That sort of horseplay just doesn't go any more. As Ambassadors of Goodwill, we are required to respect our hosts. I suppose back when you served, way back then, it was okay for the troops to behave poorly, it bein' wartime and so forth."

"Yes—yes, I guess there is a difference," I stammered.

They stood about me—young, fresh-faced, good-natured, offending no one, spending freely, amusing my little daughter as if she were a little sister—and it was with difficulty that I stifled a tear. When I shuffled off, the Texan was organizing an integrated water polo game.

That evening there was a great religious celebration—the *festa* in honor of the Virgin of Mont'Allegre. There was to be a procession, a concert, fireworks. The sailors swarmed through the streets, happy in a quiet, curious way, laden with cameras, over-priced souvenirs and shy smiles, imbibing weak beer, and still being ceremoniously ignored by the Rapallese. Indeed, it was as if our lads were *invisible*. Two dozen of them would gather in a group on a street corner to watch the procession—and the good burghers (the German term goes well with Rapallese) would avoid them as if they had no substantive existence.

There were still no officers in evidence. I wanted to race up and down the streets, shouting: "Come out, come out, wherever you are!" I never did find any.

However, I settled for two leathery Navy Chiefs, stationed somewhat conspicuously, I thought, on the intersection of Rapallo's two main streets. They had an adventurous look in their eyes, and at last, I expected to find some of the old get-up-and-go.

"Looking for excitement, men?" I asked.

They eyed me frigidly. The last thing I had intended, was to sound like a pander, but that was undoubtedly the way my question had emerged.

"You kiddin', Mac?" the older one asked. He had a purple face and was short and stout. Gold hash marks made a ladder up to his shoulder.

"No sir," the other added. "Don't catch us messin' with this foreign stuff. Got me a wife and four kids back in Naples." This fellow was a beanpole, with the floppy ears and enlarged Adam's apple of a mountain man.

"Guess you're right," I muttered—and started to walk off. To my surprise, the short one called me back.

"Pssst—Mac. You need gasoline?"

"Gasoline?" I asked.

"Yeah," the beanpole said. "*Benzina*. Petrol. You lookin' for good American gasoline, we got it to sell, at a fair price. Heck of a lot less than the ginnies charge for it."

I halted. "You mean—like you're in business on the side?" I asked.

"Might call it that," the slender one said, winking at his companion. "G'wan—tell me what you pay for gas hyeah. I'll do better, I guarantee."

It took me a little while to make the computations—litres to gallons, lire to dollars, then allow for the tourist deduction. "Oh, about sixty cents a gallon for regular."

"Well hain't that a shame," the short one said. "Me an' Chief here'll cut that price. We git it from the government for sixteen cents a gallon. You make us an offer, we'll roll a few drums to yoah house direckly." Since I did not respond at once, he let his scout's eye roam the street. "Nevah did see a dead place lak this. Can't sell a drop of stuff, and we sure got it to sell."

"And it's damn fine gas," the other added. "Navy Stores, the best. We been cleanin' up in Naples. Figured this cruise would really set us up."

At last I had found the ultimate destination of my tax dollar. All such interludes are educational. Now I knew where all that money I gave the Internal Revenue Bureau from my earnings on *The Last Angry Man* had gone. These funds, rightfully, had gone to supply gasoline at sixteen cents the gallon to our brave lads overseas, our bulwark against the Soviets. And it pleased me further that a wise, paternal government, had thus permitted these two old salt porks to branch out in business for themselves —in the best free enterprise tradition.

"Shoot," the mountain man said. "We got holt of some rich Limey down in Salerno. Fellah with a dang Rolls-Royce. Man, we kept that Limey in high-octane petrol all last yeah."

They both laughed.

"Well, I'm sorry men," I said apologetically. "But I only have

195

a small French car, and besides I don't have any place to store the drums. But if I hear about anybody who needs gasoline, I'll be sure to recommend you."

"You do that," the short one called after me. "Me an' Chief'll be at a back table at the Nettuno. We got no objections to furriners for customers, so long as they got the money."

In the warm Rapallese night, nostalgia enveloped me. As I shelled out lire to buy a plastic set of dishes for Nancy and two guaranteed breakable celluloid pop-guns for the boys, memories of other wartime entrepreneurs crowded in. Sixteen years ago I had known other visionaries like the two gasoline merchants: a Master Sergeant who retired for life on the sale of spare parts; a Captain who had done a thriving trade in automobiles commandeered from Japanese internees; a group of hospital orderlies who cornered the market in penicillin; a Warrant Officer in North Africa who was the self-proclaimed king of the mattress ticking traffic with the Arabs!

Something precious had not been lost. Perhaps the majority of the boys had changed—for the better, I am reluctantly forced to admit. Now they came into foreign ports laden with Rolleis and Voigtlanders; polite, pleasant lads, eager to please, wary of misbehavior. But among a select group of old-timers—like my two gas peddling Chiefs—the old spark burned.

Later we stood among the pink-cheeked boys on a crowded Rapallo street, and watched the holy procession in honor of the Virgin of Mont'Allegre. It was a lovely, warm evening; the happiness of *la festa* imbued all. We laughed, as a gang of schoolboys, in what I can only describe—without ridicule or condescension—as the true Italian feeling for its clergy, set off strings of violent firecrackers under a priest's cassock. He was a young, bespectacled priest, evidently their teacher, and accustomed to pranks. The boys would sneak up behind him, drop the sputtering fireworks and then race away. As they exploded, the priest, howling, would leap high, his cassock flapping. There was no disrespect in what the boys did; and no real anger in the Father. The sailors watched the charade—puzzled, outraged, laughing with the kids.

The parade began. It was the first we had seen in Italy, and it was impressive, touching. There were little girls in virginal white; older girls in colored jumpers; war veterans bemedalled with memories of the Piave, Addis Ababa (how sad!); a multitude of altar boys, seminarians, priests, Monsignori, Bishops, and the Cardinal of Genoa. The bright robes glittered, the Latin faces beamed. And there were the enormous crucifixes—huge, heavy gilt crosses with their giant Christs (one, oddly, of black wood) and as the bearers would stagger and balance their burdens, other young men stood by to relieve them.

The sky was frantic with fireworks—a Ligurian specialty. They were more dazzling, more deafening than any I have ever seen. And suddenly, in the soft Mediterranean night, a sweet, sad music settled over everything. It covered the marchers, the narrow street, the young American sailors, like a gentle musical blanket; its soft lilt even made the fireworks stop. It was the thin sound of the Rapallo town band, parading behind the giant Christs—clarinets and trombones and coronets and mandolins— solemnly played by elderly, hesitant men in white peaked caps, royal blue shirts and yellow ties. They marched poorly and fretfully, but their music was a joy. My ears still hear that wistful, reedy melody. The cadence was slow, befitting a sacred occasion; the old men treaded lightly on the asphalt.

"That tune sounds familiar," I said to Marie.

"It doesn't sound Italian," she said. "At least it isn't Neapolitan —I'd know it."

"It's beautiful," I said. "It's like Chartres. It makes you want to believe."

The sailors were more perceptive than I was. Around us, faintly, I heard the well-behaved Navy men singing the lyrics— the original American lyrics to the stately march that the Rapallo town band was playing to honor the Virgin. The young voices rose high and sweet in the night air.

> *With someone like you, a pal good and true,*
> *I'd like to leave it all behind, and go and find*
> *Some place that's known to God alone,*
> *Just a spot to call our own.*
> *We'll find a perfect peace, where joys never cease,*
> *Out there beneath a kindly sky,*
> *We'll build a sweet little nest*
> *Somewhere in the west,*
> *And let the rest of the world go by!*

The wonders of acculturation! We were all singing now—not meanly or mockingly or noisily—but with the same innocence with which the town band played the refrain.

The evening remains one of my most poignant recollections of Rapallo.

CHAPTER fourteen

all aboard for
La Dolce Vita!

August died, and with its passing our disastrous four months on the enchanted Italian Riviera ended.

There was still no P.T.A. in Portofino. But the *Che Puzza* River yet trickled by our windows, laden with potato peelings and eggshells. Above us, *Il Dottor* Nardulli, the Milanese textile broker and his family, padded about softly in stocking feet, frustrated by my refusal to recognize *zoccoli*. Now and then Officer Lentini would drop by to snoop, grub cigarettes, present me with a fresh egg, inquire about my writing, or slip me the latest gossip on Legs. Dear, dear Legs, with her mile-high thighs, was still bringing home foreign dignitaries as part of her personal people-to-people program. But she abided by Mama's bigoted rule—no representatives of the emerging nations.

And now we were off to Rome. The children were browned, peppered with bug bites, and fat with *pasta*. They were still surly. We promised Nancy lots of American friends in Rome (she got them). We promised David a new cat (he got one). We promised Teddy nothing, since he demanded nothing. Some day he will learn that there is no profit in being an uncomplaining child. And some day his mother and father will have to do something grand for Theodore Samuel Green, the deep one. In that spring and summer of bad luck, crowded beaches, overpriced villas and recalcitrant plumbing, Teddy earned his stripes. Without him, and without Mavis, we might easily have kicked the whole project and scurried back to Westbury, Long Island, like cowards.

But we were brave. We found a large, comfortable apartment in north Rome, and on September 1, we began a joyful, rewarding residence there that lasted for fourteen months. There is no point in indulging in graceless self-congratulations about our Roman sojourn. It was splendid in every way. Rome is good. Rome is sunny. Rome is a small, beautiful, accessible, warm city. Those who do not like Rome had best look to their own failings. One arrives, moves into one's apartment, villa or hotel—and the city takes over. In a few hours you have the feeling you have lived in Rome for a year already, know it, love it, and never want to leave.

We travelled a lot in the months that followed, and saw virtually all of Italy. And we learned the truth of William Styron's observation that no one—*no one*—can possibly give more to Italy than he gets from it. We hope we were good visitors—as good as the cheerful American tourists we met everywhere. We learned, we observed, we were awed, and we made many friends. Italy possesses a soothing magic—a compound of art and architecture and history and landscape and good food and sun and the general amiability of its people. One loses one's temper daily with the Italians, and ends up surrendering to them and loving them. I'm not sure why this is: Italians are probably no more virtuous or lovable than other people. Essentially, I think that their attractiveness stems from their talent for making the most of their lives—and 90 per cent of Italian lives are poor, insecure and stratified. Yet I know of no people on earth who get so much mileage out of their allotted hours. Far be it from me to perpetuate the myth of the happy poor. Too well I remember Incoronata and her family in Massadonia—and Sicily and Calabria, which we visited later. I merely say that the capacity to live, to take pleasure in the minutiae of life, is high among them.

And eventually, this talent infects confirmed pessimists—like myself. It is difficult to explain the joy I felt one sunny day, motoring near Bologna and temporarily lost on a back road, when Nancy leaned from the window of the car and shouted—in flawless colloquial Italian—at a road laborer:

"*Senti! Dov'è la strada per Faenza?*—Listen! Where's the road to Faenza?"

And he, gnarled, sun-seared, dirty, under-paid, and in all probability a Communist (the Bologna area is extremely Red) laughed and shouted back the instructions—scratching his coarse head at the improbability of a French car, an Italian-speaking child, and an English-speaking father who looked like a German. (To Italian eyes, I am almost always German. Something in their wry vision filters out the Middle-Eastern in me and renders me Aryan).

For a poor country, it is amazing the way one finds affirmation everywhere. I suppose much of this, this strong affirmative voice amid poverty, is the spell cast by a magnificent past—perpetual reminders of man's infinite capacity to create. In Spoleto we stood in the ancient cathedral and stared hypnotically at the inspired frescoes in the apse—four scenes from the life of the Virgin. We didn't have the guide book that day, and we weren't smart enough to know the artist, but we knew we were in the presence of grandeur.

"Maybe Della Francesca," I ventured.

"Or Perugino?" Marie asked.

A sexton in black smock came limping out of the shadows; we were the only ones in the church and he had heard our voices. *"Per carità, Signor,"* he said, chiding us, "don't you know Lippo Lippi when you see him?"

Masterpieces they were; and our ignorance didn't embarrass us. We were too happy at finding Fra Lippo Lippi. Back in Rome, I hurried to the American Library to read Browning again, on the great Florentine.

> *If you get simple beauty and naught else,*
> *You get about the best thing God invents.*

When we had nourished our spirits sufficiently with the frescoes, the sexton led us to a locked chapel, opened it, and revealed a bonus of unexpected delight—two Pinturicchios!

This, of course, is not a travel guide. But I cannot help but recall more of the affirmative Italy—the Greek temples at Paestum, below Salerno, stunning the viewer with their absolute grace, their majestic proportions; the frescoed tombs of Tarquinia, those Etruscan celebrations of life, brighter than daylight; the Pompeiian bronzes in the neglected archaeological museum of Naples. All these and scores of others were part of a texture, a tactile experience, a web of light and color and form and achievement, that would often require me to hide tears of happiness behind my army surplus glasses, when we emerged into the flooding sun. It has been done before, I would tell myself, why can't it be done again? Or even approximated.

These memories have size and form and are multi-hued: Marie and myself and our children sitting in a restaurant in the Piazza in Orvieto, that enchanted hill city, sipping the fragrant wine that bears its name, staring, dazzled at the soaring, lacy facade, the four needlesharp towers of the Cathedral. Sensations mesh, harmonize, induce in us a hopefulness, a belief in a grand artistic continuum. (One need not accept the dogma, incidentally, to love the art; I have found Italian churchmen most tolerant on this matter.) I see our three children scampering up and down the steps of the Orvieto Cathedral, happy with a new tourist bauble they have won for good behavior. Above them rise the brilliant mosaics, the intricate stone-work, and above the spires, is the pure blue sky and the high, gentle sun—as subtle as the aroma of Orvieto wine. All these make up the texture of a moment, the threads of a rich fabric that unrolls across centuries, across national origins, and parochial beliefs.

Is it irrelevant, I have asked myself, that the Italians, under the heel of a Fascist government, allied with the German madman, too often denigrated as without courage or principle, possess one of the bravest records in Europe in the matter of protecting Jews from the depraved murderers of the North? Long before the Eichmann trial I heard this testimony to Italian decency—not from the Italians, who brag very little about their national virtues, but from an Israeli cabinet minister I met in Rome! All of us appreciate virtue in those we like; and this evidence of good deeds, of eminent decency in the Italians delighted me.

And so, we let Rome and Italy adopt us. The boys wore tight shorts and knee-length socks. On Sunday afternoons they kicked a soccer ball about the Piazza Navona. Nancy found an Italian replacement for Janet—not an American, but a fanciful, imaginative Italian boy named Giancarlo. He lived in the apartment below us, a handsome, pale, sleepy child, forever yawning because of too many siestas and long nocturnal TV watching. He was always dressed in shorts, suspenders and fuzzy lambswool slippers, and apparently never went out of doors. I often expected to see a cigarette dangling from his mouth. But he was a good and gentle friend to Nancy for many months.

As for myself, I feverishly sought *La Dolce Vita*.

"I was square in Westbury and cubed in Rapallo," I told Marie. "But all that is behind me. Now I am off to Rome—the heir to centuries of decadent sophistication. Beware. I am an American writer and I am entitled to this sort of thing."

How I looked forward to plunging into that mad whirl of corruption! Now that Portofino and Rapallo, and Mr. Fodor's infectiously gay, *chi-chi* ambience had somehow eluded me, I would more than make up for it in Rome.

Yet—somehow it all eluded me again.

I tried manfully to find that sweet, sinful life, but I never found it. For some reason, the sidewalk cafes on the Via Veneto that we frequented, even late at night, were forever devoid of actors, decadent aristocrats, *invertiti*, or lady professionals. Generally, we were surrounded by smiling Americans eating ice-cream. Once I thought I saw an actress, but she was only a house-wife from Aurora, Illinois, in a Marshall Field dress.

We even went so far as to spend a summer in Fregene, a resort near Rome, which is the site of Mr. Fellini's most decadent, vicious assembly of no-goods. We were in Fregene two months. We never attended such a party. We never heard of one—and we knew several theatrical people, Italians and Americans. We never even saw anyone who *looked* like they were getting ready to have such a terrible party, or had just come from one. The most immoral thing that happened all summer was when our cesspool overflowed.

If anything, Rome had a retrograde effect on my search for sin. In Westbury, Long Island, I had been the neighborhood crank. I boycotted P.T.A. meetings, I let my lawn grow rank with weeds, I refused to wash my car. But Rome changed all that. The third day after I arrived, I was unanimously elected chairman of the Overseas School of Rome's Building Dedication Committee. I found myself the only male at committee meetings; I helped draw up the program for Dedication Day. Soon, the headmaster's wife had me chaperoning sub-teen dances. I was appointed advertising chairman for the school's souvenir pro-gram at its annual Christmas Ball. Proudly, I can report that we made record profits at the 1959 dance. That almost made up for all those Fellini-type parties I missed—the Overseas School is a superb school, and needed the money.

Rome was so good, that even our memories of Rapallo seemed pleasanter. Even memories of Officer Lentini, who somehow would not leave us, even though 300 miles away.

We had made our hegira to Rome in two stages. I had driven down with Nancy and Filomena, who had agreed to stay with us for a week until we hired another maid. Marie followed the next day on the express train, with the boys and a few valises. She arrived an hour late, weeping.

"The big valise was stolen," she said. "It had all my jewelry in it—all my good summer dresses."

The usual scene followed. I was my normal tolerant self, bawling her out for leaving the suitcase unattended. We reported it to the railway police.

"Impossible, *Signor* Gren," their chief said. "Valises are never stolen from Italian trains."

There followed two days of tears, ill temper, and a gnawing realization that we would never see a lira's worth of insurance. Since we no longer had an American house, we no longer had insurance on it—and we no longer had the rider that covered us in transit. We did have an Italian policy, but it did not include (we learned after the valise vanished) thefts in transit, theft at temporary residences, theft by domestics, accidental loss, or loss due to earthquake, tidal wave, volcanic eruption or armed insurrection.

We resigned ourself to a dead loss. Perhaps some day we would wander through the Rome Flea Market at the Porta Portuense, and see again some of our irreplaceables—a free-form brooch set with a taxidermist's cat's eye that I bought from Sam Kramer in Greenwich Village; a fake Navajo bracelet from a Las Vegas gift shop; the intra-mural softball medal I won in 1941 at Columbia College, the year I batted .489 for a championship team named the Royal Elite Cuban Giants.

Two days later, the chief of the railroad police called on us. Even for a Roman cop, his manner was agitated. He was performing little entre-chatisses in our lobby, clapping his hands, rolling his liquid brown eyes.

"A miracle! A miracle!" he cried. "We have found *La Signora's* valise!"

A nation of absolutes and impossibilities: two days before, the same man had informed us that valises were never stolen. Now, he was even more emphatic in stating that ours was the first valise ever recovered.

"What luck! What good fortune!" the railway policeman shouted. "An Englishman took the valise off the train by mistake in Livorno. At the hotel, this fool discovered his error and called the local police. They searched the bag, and now the greatest miracle of all—" He clasped his chubby hands beneath his chin. "In the valise, the police found a letter addressed to *Signor* Gren in Rapallo. A telephone call was made to Rapallo. Can you guess who responded?"

"A man named Lentini," I said wearily. Truly, there was no escape from *Il Rompere-Coglioni*.

"Exactly! Your esteemed neighbor and friend. I have since spoken with this Officer Lentini. A man of parts—"

"Private parts," I muttered in English.

"Gerald!" Marie reprimanded. So happy was she in squirming off the hook of neglect, she was going on the offensive.

"A splendid fellow, Lentini, Angelo," the chief continued. "He naturally had your Rome address and gave it to the Livorno police, with a description of you and your family. When I spoke to him, he disclosed that he is collaborating with you on a book on Italian police methods. He also sends word that your repeated complaints have moved the city to clean out a body of water called, humorously, the *Che Puzza* River. Moreover, he asked me to tell you that a certain young lady upstairs has run off with a Nationalist Chinese General to Majorca."

At once we drove to the Rome station—the three children,

and David's new cat included. We identified the valise, as four more cops grinned their delight. It was a triumph shared by all —an augury of a good time to come.

As we left the police office, an elderly porter, shoving a hand car offered the children rides. We dumped the prodigal valise, Nancy, Teddy, David and the new cat on the cart, and walked down the long, wide platform. Sunlight streamed through the roof above the tracks. The porter was a Neapolitan, and Marie talked to him in dialect.

I could hardly envision a similar scene in Penn Station. Undoubtedly there are rules against children and cats riding hand cars. And the porters with whom I have attempted to converse regard me with uniform suspicion, if not downright enmity. (I know, they have *their* problems—but I'm only trying to be nice.)

At the parking lot, I tipped the porter, and we drove off. Opposite a stretch of venerable olive-drab wall, I slowed down.

"That, children," I said, "is one of the oldest walls in Rome. It is perhaps 2500 years old." It seemed a good time to begin their classical education.

"Is it older than you?" Teddy asked.

"Not much," answered Nancy.

David sleepily hugged his cat—a white derelict with crafty amber eyes.

The Romans paraded about in Sunday finery—shopgirls, secretaries and clerks as well-dressed as any Contessa or Barone. Sparkling Fiats and Lancias whizzed by—no one cleans his car the way a Roman does. The September sky was hot, clear and dry. Now I knew why Romans favor fruit shades for their buildings—melon, apricot, tangerine. The colors startle and dazzle against that Perugino blue.

"Is it reaching you?" I asked Marie.

"If it didn't, there'd be something wrong with me," she said. "I'm getting the shivers."

We drove to the Palatine. I read aloud from Giuseppi Lugli's guide book, while the children played tag in the ruins of Domitian's stadium. In the dry, healing sunlight, amid cypresses, parasol pines and the old stones and bricks, we let Rome adopt us.

She is an indulgent and generous mother—like most Italian mothers. Soothed, I unfroze my heart sufficiently to think a few kind thoughts about Rapallo and Portofino.

Some day I shall go back there and organize a P.T.A.